Humanistic Studies in the Communication Arts

GEORGE N. GORDON · General Editor

COMMUNICATION ARTS
IN THE ANCIENT WORLD

Humanistic Studies in the Communication Arts

A TAXONOMY OF
CONCEPTS IN COMMUNICATION
by Reed H. Blake and Edwin O. Haroldsen

COMMUNICATIONS AND MEDIA
Constructing a Cross Discipline
by George N. Gordon

ETHICS AND THE PRESS
Readings in Mass Media Morality
Edited by John C. Merrill and Ralph D. Barney

DRAMA IN LIFE
The Uses of Communication in Society
Edited by James E. Combs and Michael W. Mansfield

INTERNATIONAL AND INTERCULTURAL COMMUNICATION
Edited by Heinz-Dietrich Fischer and John C. Merrill

EXISTENTIAL JOURNALISM
by John C. Merrill

THE COMMUNICATIONS REVOLUTION
A History of Mass Media in the United States
by George N. Gordon

COMMUNICATION ARTS IN THE ANCIENT WORLD
Edited by Eric A. Havelock and Jackson P. Hershbell

H|S
C|A   *Humanistic Studies in the Communication Arts*

COMMUNICATION ARTS IN THE ANCIENT WORLD

Edited by

ERIC A. HAVELOCK and

JACKSON P. HERSHBELL

COMMUNICATION ARTS BOOKS

HASTINGS HOUSE · PUBLISHERS

New York 10016

LIBRARY OF CONGRESS CATALOGING IN PUBLICATION DATA

Main entry under title:

Communication arts in the ancient world.

   (Humanistic studies in the communication arts)
(Communication arts books)
     Includes bibliographical references and index.
     1. Communication—Greece—History—Addresses, essays,
lectures. 2. Communication—Rome—History—Addresses,
essays, lectures. I. Havelock, Eric Alfred.
II. Hershbell, Jackson P., 1935–
P92.G75C65   301.14'0937   78-17482
ISBN 0-8038-1252-3

Published simultaneously in Canada by
Copp Clark Ltd., Toronto

Printed in the United States of America

Contents

Foreword

THE FORMAL STUDY of communications, interpersonal or mass (along with computer science), is one of the newest fields of intellectual endeavor on the Western marketplace of ideation. As a discipline, or cross-discipline as I have suggested elsewhere, it has not yet withstood a test of time and durability the way most of our other scholarly pursuits have, some well and some poorly. Witchcraft, for instance, is rarely taught any longer on most university campuses, and sociology is, although the intellectual roots of the former are enmeshed more complexly with our intellectual tradition by time and custom than are the latter. I am on intimate terms with only one witch, and, it seems to me, she has developed a more realistic attitude towards the fads and fashions of scholarship than most sociologists I know. "It had its day, and it will again," says my philosophical necromancer.

Communication studies as a discipline has not yet "had its day." Nor did such a discipline even exist when I was young during the depression years. It was not until 1970 or so, in fact, that the editors of the *Encyclopedia Britannica* sent me a fancy letter requesting that I write an article on the subject for their latest edition—not too long, either, and certainly not to exceed 10,000 words. My piece in their *Macropaedia* of their fifteenth edition is therefore, I imagine, something of a landmark, although I cannot claim in any sense that I made history. Intellectual history merely caught up with me—and the *Britannica*'s computers—and, about ten years after most universities in America started gathering faculties of communications, the baby was officially baptized and given a category of its own by the keepers of the *Britannica*'s flame. (I think it is interesting that the usually well written and illustrated article in previous *Britannica* editions on the "Art of Conjuring and Performing Magic" was dropped entirely in the fifteenth edition after many, many years.)

Of course, the word "communication" has been in general currency since the days of Rome in one version or another, as Professor Hershbell notes in the pages just ahead. But emphasis in definition has usually been placed upon the content of messages, and media, if at all relevant, have been relegated to adverbial statements like "by means of smoke signals." What brought the *process* of communication to the attention of so many people and started them asking so many questions about it—some good, some bad, and some silly—was the growing role that contemporary technology has played in the West by introducing near unending streams of novel devices to cover distances and preserve in time galaxies of communications content that were once severely limited by the dual tyrannies of space and the passing moment. The result, on one hand, was telecommunications, and, on the other, photography, recording and other devices that deep-freeze a communication and preserve its form and integrity. It is no accident that inroads into the theoretical aspects of these phenomena were originally proposed by scientists working for a telephone company, involved in, among other things, sound recording.

In a short time, however, and some time before that benevolent nod from the *Britannica* people, those of us caught up in studies of what we were calling "communications" by the 1950's had, to mix a metaphor, discovered that we had opened Pandora's Box and found a hydra-headed monster in it. Here was a game anybody could play, and the "anybodys" included contemporary gnostics from Canada, linguists and semanticists of various persuasions, moralists (who kept muttering things about "audiovisual education") and enormous covens of sociologists and psychologists armed with models and statistical readouts, as well as unemployed movie critics and others. Among them also was a clutch of historians. But, because of the immediacy of the flashy technology that fascinated nearly all of these seekers after truth, a biographical study of the cultural influence of the art of Warner Baxter might well be considered history, and an article on the travails of Thomas Nast's career was regarded as *ancient* history.

As we enter the second phase of the study of the communication arts and sciences, I think that those of us professionally involved in this cross-discipline have, by the pressure of experience, been forced into a new and hopeful humility. Twenty or thirty years ago we (or our teachers) were comparatively restless in our interests, and it was perfectly natural—and human—for us to waste most of our fascination upon the galaxy of new technology that was, as far as we could figure out, changing societal ground rules of the present moment and hurling into a disconnected future unrelated either to tradition or history. We had not learned what we have found out since: that all new techniques and technologies produce similar auras of uniqueness, novelty and disconnection and that, regardless of this illusion, man's social and personal conditions remain remarkably constant in the face of continual cultural variations, usually mislabeled "revolutions."

This is the intellectual reason that I welcome so eagerly the classical scholars who follow in this book to the *Humanistic Studies in the Communication Arts*. The focus of their special interest is upon a revealing (and dangerous) period in the Western scientific and artistic tradition, the period when those people we call "the ancients" moved, not from an oral tradition but a *number* of them, in different ways and for different reasons, not into *one* written tradition but a *number* of them, with and without, as the reader will see, pictographic (or visual) assistance. They center upon a period of technical change in human communication that rivals our own in diversity and pith, and from which we modernists can learn much of both theoretical and practical immediate importance.

Let me admit, however, that my delight in seeing *Communication Arts in the Ancient World* in print is more than intellectual. That this collection has been gathered by so eminent a team of classicists as Professors Havelock and Hershbell, and that they have interested so superb a group of writers (with one exception) in adding their efforts to this venture both excites and pleases me. Many of my colleagues in older disciplines, correctly I think, have been skeptical about the *bona fides* of many of us who claim expertise in so-called "communications", largely because of the abnormal quantum of charlatons, conmen and double-talk experts who have, since the early 'sixties, received too much attention from journalists of print and television motived by cold blooded exploitation. They have also had to witness the humiliation of other, mercifully few, academics who fell for these frauds, because they offered fancy, catchphrases for commonplaces and pseudo-theories that they thought made sense because they were impossible to understand.

This period of nasty deception seems now to be over. I think that the publication of this book, speaking in the civil and scholarly manner of classical investigation and directed, in part at least, to those of us immersed in the technology of modernity is, therefore, an important step towards building a bridge between scholars whose common central interest in human communications is delimited neither by time nor culture nor doctrine, but who, often and mistakenly, think of their fundamental concerns as unrelated one to the other. Precisely how wrong they are is the unspoken theme of every essay in this volume.

GEORGE N. GORDON

Introduction

WESTERN CULTURE is without doubt a literate one—the alphabet has existed for some 2900 years, a large number of people can read and write, and a vast print and pulp technology reinforces habits of literacy. There also exists, at least in the West, a widespread assumption that literate cultures are somehow superior to non-literate ones, and that the latter usually collapse before the approach of what are considered to be more civilized ways of life. It is thus often thought that the ancient Greeks and Romans, because of their highly civilized, efficient, and by then standards, technological societies, must have been highly literate. That the first "literature" of the Western world, the Homeric epics, was orally composed, or that the creators of the Parthenon were perhaps semi-literate, are views that have not always found favor among literate students of antiquity. Only "barbarians," like Theodoric the Ostrogoth (king of Italy, 493–526 A. D.), were so illiterate that they could not even write their own names. The Greeks and Romans, however, understood *anakoinōsis* or *communicatio* to mean the process of informing not only by writing, but also by speaking, and they were aware of the novelty of writing; see, for example, Aeschylus, *Prometheus Bound* 455 f., or Plato, *Phaedrus* 274b f. It should also not be forgotten that "silent" reading was rare in antiquity, and that "books" were produced manually by scribes—printing did not come into existence until the fifteenth century A. D.

This volume is primarily devoted to exploring the beginnings of literacy in ancient Greece and Rome, and the effects of writing on these cultures. In "The Alphabetization of Homer," E. A. Havelock discusses the impact of the alphabet's introduction on the Homeric epics, and compares in some detail Greek (Homeric) and Mesopotamian flood stories—cuneiform (syllabary) vs. the alphabet. His observations on the "psychology" of oral composition are especially interesting, e. g. the "echo principle" and its effects. Havelock describes at length the superiority of the alphabet over previous writing systems, and concludes with a brief analysis of the tensions between oral and written transmission.

In "The Poetic Sources of the Greek Alphabet," K. Robb engages in a comparative study of the earliest Greek and Phoenician inscriptions. According to him, about 750 B. C. the Greeks brought into existence "the world's first complete alphabet," borrowing a script from their Phoenician neighbors not for the purpose of keeping account of business transactions, but for recording Greek oral verse on some enduring substance. Attention is given to the contrasts between Greek and Semitic poetry, and, in general, Robb offers a study that is fascinating and provocative.

J. Russo deals with the composition of the Homeric epics, circa the eighth-seventh centuries B. C., and though he doubts that Homeric poetry was truly oral, it was nonetheless "aural." His discussion of the epic outlook, and the notion that Greek epic poetry was created to function as an effective medium of communication, primarily in an oral culture, explains much of the strangeness of Homer to a modern literary guild. For Russo the epic language is a special kind of language, and the epic outlook uses the spoken word to construct a world (not word) picture.

G. Gordon argues persuasively that the origins of propaganda are not in the print technology of the sixteenth and seventeenth centuries, but in ancient Greece, and that the Aristotelian *enthymeme* is at the heart of persuasion. According to Gordon, the "living, spoken word is a better vehicle for persuasion than print, recordings or simulations of any type," and this was fully realized by Aristotle.

In an article which may, at first glance, seem somewhat technical, F. D. Harvey examines in detail the small literary evidence that remains of how the Greeks and Romans actually learned to write. It is interesting to note that, according to Harvey, technology in the ancient world moved at a very leisurely pace, and teaching methods, at least in the Roman world, remained unchanged for several centuries. Letters in the form of toys and writing elephants (!) are some amusing curiosities Harvey has discovered in the course of his research which is a valuable contribution to the history of education as well as communication.

My study on the ancient telegraph underscores Harvey's observation that technological development was slow in the ancient world. What technological development there was, was often in connection with war. Certainly this seems true of the telegraph—that there was one in the ancient world may surprise modern readers. Because of various technological problems, however, it was never used widely, and there seems to be a correlation between the rise and spread of literacy, and the development of the telegraph, literally "writing at a distance."

The fascinating studies of C. M. Havelock and E. Keuls focus in different ways on the role of visual art in communication. Accepting the view that the early Greeks were semi-literate at best, Havelock examines some of the "messages" contained in the medium of the visual arts, temples and sculpture. Battle scenes, for example, were quite common, and Havelock views these as messages to Greek youths to fight bravely and dauntlessly. She analyzes not only the effect of subject matter in Greek art, but also the manner of execution, e.g. the visual brightness and lifelike quality of the objects depicted. This too was part of the "message."

Keuls' article on rhetoric and the use of visual aids is based mainly on literary evidence. The visual aids themselves no longer remain, but that they were used by the Sophists, for example, to convey messages or to enhance an oral presentation, seems clear. Keuls also gives some insights into the art of persuasion as practiced in the Homeric world as well as in the later Greco-Roman period. Despite the different kinds of evidence on which they are based, the contributions of C. M. Havelock and Keuls stress the importance of visual techniques in ancient communication.

The study of Gentili and Cerri shows the effect of literacy on Greek historical writing, and it is a good analysis of the conflict between the aims of essentially oral narration and those of written communication in the reconstruction of the past. The authors view this problem beginning with Herodotus, "the father of history" (fifth century B. C.), down to later and lesser known historians such as Timaeus of Tauromenium (second century B. C.). That the nature of historiography remains a perennial problem is well illustrated by the authors' references to works such as E. H. Carr, *What is History?*

The articles in this volume have been written with classicist and non-classicist in mind. "Little Latin and less Greek" are required for understanding the contributions which are often illustrative of some of the problems involved in understanding the past, e. g. the fragmentary or incomplete nature of some of the evidence. It is hoped that above all, these studies will be of value not only to students of the Greco-Roman world, but also to those attempting to understand the present. No doubt the implications of these studies for modern discussions of communication are best drawn by the readers. This volume makes it clear, of course, that the beginnings of Western civilization are in the spoken, not written or printed word, and that a culture can be highly efficient and "civilized" without widespread literacy. Moreover, oral and literate cultures often have quite different attitudes to the world and to history as is shown in the studies of E. A. Havelock, Russo, and Gentili and Cerri. In addition to students of communication, those interested in art history, the history of education, historical writing, literature, anthropology, and rhetoric, will find much of interest in this volume.

I would like to thank my fellow editor and contributor, Eric Havelock, for his enormous help and encouragement in preparing this volume. Special thanks are also due to George Gordon for his continuing interest and judicious advice.

JACKSON P. HERSHBELL

Humanistic Studies in the Communication Arts

GEORGE N. GORDON · General Editor

COMMUNICATION ARTS
IN THE ANCIENT WORLD

The career of ERIC A. HAVELOCK has spanned two continents, three countries and six universities. Born in London in 1903 and resident during his boyhood in the north of Scotland, he gained his degree at Cambridge (a "Double First" with special Distinction in Ancient Philosophy). Three years of apprenticeship in Nova Scotia were followed by sixteen more at the University of Toronto where in addition to playing an active and innovative role in the teaching curriculum he found time to publish his first book, to found one periodical and serve as an associate editor of another, and to run unsuccessfully for a seat in the Ontario legislature. When the Guggenheim Fellowships were opened to residents of Canada, he was among the earliest winners. Called to Harvard in 1947, he was soon invited to participate in the General Education programme, then recently established. His management of the basic course known in those days as "Humanities One" is still recalled by former students. A stint at the Chairmanship of the Classics Department was followed by a year as Visiting Professor at Princeton. By 1963, having published three more books Havelock had reached the age of sixty, and now faced an invitation from the Yale administration to come to New Haven as Sterling Professor and Chairman to assist in the reorganization of the Yale Classics Department. The assignment when reluctantly accepted made him presumably the only teacher to have served both Harvard and Yale in this capacity. Retirement from Yale was followed by two years as Raymond Professor at the State University of New York at Buffalo.

Havelock, with some justice, has been styled the "Odysseus" of his profession; it has been said of his books that they are written a generation in advance of their time. The first which appeared on the bookshelves about the time that Hitler invaded Poland, was later described, in *Fifty Years of Classical Scholarship* in the following terms: "In 1939 . . . *The Lyric Genius of Catullus* swept like a gust of fresh air through the stuffy corridors of Catullian criticism . . . Such a challenge to familiar views even if too provocative for general acceptance, at least earns the credit due to those who refresh the mind by suggesting new answers to old questions . . . certainly no teacher could wish for a more stimulating book to put into the hands of present day students."

Several of his articles published in recent years have concentrated on the Greeks in their role, as he argues, as the inventors of European literacy. Readers of his *Preface to Plato* (1963) will recognize the pertinence of that work to the article he has contributed to the present volume. Married twice, Professor Havelock has three children, all authors themselves, and ten grandchildren, and has just completed his fifth book.

The Alphabetization
of Homer[1]

by ERIC A. HAVELOCK

SOMEWHERE between 700 and 550 B.C. the *Iliad* and the *Odyssey* were as we say "committed to writing." This way of putting it describes an operation which under modern conditions occurs ten thousand times an hour all over the literate world. The original act was rather different; it was something like a thunder-clap in human history, which our bias of familiarity has converted into the rustle of papers on a desk. It constituted an intrusion into culture, with results that proved irreversible. It laid the basis for the destruction of the oral way of life and the oral modes of thought. This is an extreme way of putting it, intended to dramatize a fact about ourselves. We as literates, inheritors of 2500 years of experience with the written word, are removed by a great distance from the conditions under which the written word first entered Greece, and it requires some effort of the imagination to comprehend what these were and how they affected the manner in which the event took place. More accurately, rather than speak of destruction, we should say that what set in with the alphabetization of Homer was a process of erosion of "orality," extending over centuries of the European experience, one which has left modern culture unevenly divided between oral and literate modes of expression, experience, and living.

All societies support and strengthen their identity by conserving their mores. A social consciousness, formed as a consensus, is as it were continually placed in storage for re-use. Literate societies do this by documentation; preliterate ones achieve the same result by the composition of poetic narratives which serve also as encyclopedias of conduct. These exist and are transmitted through memorization, and as continually recited constitute a report—a reaffirmation—of the communal ethos and also a recommendation to abide by it. Such were the Homeric poems, enclaves of contrived language existing alongside the vernacular. Their contrivance was a response to the rules of oral memorization and the need for secure transmission. Linguistic statements could be remembered and repeated only as they were specially shaped: they existed solely as sound, memorized through the ears and practiced by the mouths of living persons. This sound-sequence was suddenly brought into contact with a set of written symbols possessed of unique phonetic efficiency. An automatic marriage occurred between the two; or, to change the metaphor, upon a body of liquid contained in a vessel was dropped a substance which crystallized the contents and precipitated a deposit upon the bottom.

The spoken and remembered word had after millennia of experimentation with devices we call "writing"—a process abandoned in Greece after the fall of Mycenae—found at last the perfect instrument for its transcription. And therefore in "Homer" we confront a paradox unique in history: two poems we can read in documented form, the first "literature" of Europe; which however constitute the first complete record of "orality," that is, "non-literature"—the only one we are ever likely to have: a statement of how civilized man governed his life and thought during several centuries when he was entirely innocent of the art (or arts) of reading.

The alphabet applied to the Homeric tongue constituted an act of "translation" from sound to sight. It is the completeness of the art which must first be emphasized, and therefore the completeness of the coverage of human experience. Phonetic efficiency meant the removal of that ambiguity of recognition which had limited all previous writing systems in their application.[2] Let us suppose—the supposition is unfounded—that knowledge and use of "Linear B" had survived into early Hellenism. The epic "report" on the Hellenic life-style and mores would have continued to be practiced and recited among the predominantly oral population. The scribes, servants of palace or temple bureaucracies, would have produced what we might call epitomes of this epic material, simplified versions accommodated to the limitations which were inherent in the difficulty of recognition and would require economy and repetitiousness of vocabulary with minimum variation in types of statement. Catalogues and quantities would abound, psychological analysis would be absent. Though meter might be retained, performance would be not popular but liturgical, reserved for high occasions. Meanwhile "Homer" would have continued in composition and recitation among the people, but with the likelihood that the quality of oral art practiced would have suffered because the linguistic brains of the community were being drained off into the scribal centers. Homer's formulaic complexity, unique among the surviving remnants of oral poetry, bespeaks a culture totally non-literate, in which a monopoly of linguistic sophistication was vested in the bard.

A flood recorded in cuneiform

We do not have any Linear B "epic" to support the hypothesis just proposed. Could it be supported by any comparison with syllabic documents of other cultures, documents, that is, which were pre-alphabetic? There is a passage in the *Epic of Gilgamesh* which achieves a degree of narrative vividness not to be matched elsewhere in the poem. This seems due to the employment of an unusually rich vocabulary of words describing acts and occurrences which are very concrete and specific—we might say detailed. Such at least would be the inference which a scholar ignorant of cuneiform—as is the present writer— would allow himself to draw from the English translation that Near Eastern scholarship has provided.[3] The narrator is one Utnapishtim, the Babylonian Noah; his account of the Flood is recognizable as the model for the parallel story in the *Book of Genesis*:

> With the first glow of dawn
> A black cloud rose up from the horizon
> Inside it Adad thunders
> While Shullat and Hanish go in front
> 5 Moving as heralds over hill and plain.
> Erragal tears out the posts;
> Forth comes Ninurta and causes the dikes to follow.
> The Anunnaki lift up the torches
> Setting the land ablaze with their glare.
> 10 Consternation over Adad reaches to the heavens,
> Who turned to blackness all that had been light.
> [The wide] land was shattered like [a pot]:
> For one day the south-storm [blew].
> Gathering speed as it blew [submerging the mountains].
> 15 Overtaking the [people] like a battle.
> No one can see his fellow,
> Nor can the people be recognized from heaven.

> The gods were frightened by the deluge,
> And shrinking back, they ascended to the heaven of Anu . . .
> 20 Six days and [six] nights
> Blows the flood wind, as the south-storm sweeps the land
> When the seventh day arrived,
> The flood [-carrying] south-storm subsided in the battle
> Which it had fought like an army,
> 25 The sea grew quiet, the tempest was still, the flood ceased.
> I looked at the weather: stillness had set in
> And all of mankind had returned to clay.
> 28 The landscape was as level as a flat roof.

What variety of vocabulary has been packed so to speak into this passage? Obviously a translation does not of itself provide an accurate word-count of the original. As a general rule it will be a little richer, indulging in the temptation to provide variants in varying contexts for what are really equivalents. However, for what it is worth, a word-count can be made: prepositions and conjunctions can be ignored, also inflections, and the names of the gods can be counted as a single unit, representing a catalogue. With these provisos, the passage in translation furnishes a total of 90 words, of which 69 are unique; the repetitions are counted as follows:

doublets: black . . . blackness (2, 11); go-in-front . . . forth-comes (4, 7); all (11, 27); battle (15, 23); people (15, 17); can (16, 17); six (20); still . . . stillness (25, 26)

triplets: land (9, 12, 21); heavens (10, 17, 19); day (13, 20, 22); blew (13, 14, 21); south-storm (13, 21, 23)

quadruplet: deluge and flood (if equivalent) (18, 21, 23, 25).

The percentage of non-unique words to the total is 23.3.

More significant (because less liable to distortion through translation) are duplicated statements, not necessarily equivalent, but expressive of meanings which paraphrase each other. This phenomenon does not occur in the first 12 lines. But then it is as though the verbal "originality" of composition begins to exhaust itself, and we get the following series of repetitive sequences:

(a) 13 for one day the south-storm blew
    14 gathering speed as it blew
    20 six days and six nights
    21 blows the flood wind as the south-storm sweeps the land
(b) 16 no one can see his fellows
    17 nor can the people be recognized
(c) 18 the gods were frightened
    19 and shrinking back
(d) 15 overtaking the people like a battle
    23 subsided in battle
    24 which it had fought like an army
(e) 25 sea grew quiet, tempest was still, flood ceased
    26 stillness had set in.

The description of the Flood is interrupted by a digression of 13 lines describing the conclave of the frightened gods. It intervenes between lines 19 and 20 of the passage as we have printed it, and runs as follows.

> The gods cowered like dogs
>> Crouched against the outer wall.
> Ishtar cried out like a woman in travail,
> The sweet-voiced mistress of the [gods] moans aloud:
> 5 "The olden days are alas turned to clay,
> Because I bespoke evil in the assembbly of the gods.
> How could I bespeak evil in the assembly of the gods,
> Ordering battle for the destruction of my people!
> When it is I myself who gives birth to my people!
> 10 Like the spawn of the fishes they fill the sea!"
> The Anunnaki gods weep with her,
> The gods, all humbled, sit and weep,
> Their lips drawn tight, [. . .] one and all.

The repetitive, not to say ritualistic character of this passage is obvious: line 7 repeats line 6; the word gods recurs six times in 12 lines; six of the verbs fall into three pairs of variants: cowered—crouched; cried out—moans aloud; weep with her—sit and weep; and there are repetitions of motifs contained in the storm passage.

A flood recorded in the alphabet

It is now appropriate to compare a description of a flood producing similar consequences as it occurs in the text of Homer. In the twelfth book of the *Iliad* the poet himself undertakes to explain why it is that the fortifications built by the Greeks to protect their camp are in his day no longer extant:

12.17 Then indeed Poseidon and Apollo devised
> the wall to demolish, by intruding the might of rivers
> as many as from Idaean mountains seaward flow-forth
> 20 Rhesus and Heptaporos and Caresus and Rhodius
> Granicus and Aesopus and divine Scamander
> and Simois, where many oxhide-shields and helmets
> tumbled in mud and the generation of demigod men;
> of them all the mouths together Phoebus Apollo turned
> 25 and nine-days against the wall directed the flow; and Zeus rained
> continually, that sooner he might set the walls sea-born;
> himself the earth-shaker having trident in hands
> went-before, and all foundations discharged upon-the-waves
> of logs and stones, that the toiling Achaeans had-set
> 30 and made [them] smooth beside full-flowing Hellespont
> and again the great foreshore covered with sand
> the wall having-demolished; the rivers he turned to run
> 33 down their flow, whereby formerly they directed [their] fair-flowing water.

Ignoring the Greek particles, counting Poseidon-Apollo as one term, but Zeus separately, and counting the river-catalogue as one, this passage provides a total of 71 words, of which 61 are unique; the repetitions being counted as follows:

doublets: demolish (18, 32); rivers (18, 32); directed (25, 33); turned
                 (24, 32); set (26, 29); flow (25, 33); all (24, 28);
one quadruplet: wall (18, 25, 26, 32).

The percentage of non-unique words to the total is 14%.

Of these two epic descriptions of similar events, the Greek one has managed a variety of vocabulary proportionately greater. The difference between 14% and 23% may not seem very great but it assumes significance when it is borne in mind that the concrete vividness of the Babylonian is untypical of what is mostly offered in the translated version of the epic, whereas the Greek passage is typical of Greek epic. When we look, in the Greek, for duplicated statements not necessarily equivalent but expressive of meanings which paraphrase each other, we discover only one:

                 18 the wall to-demolish
                 32 the wall having-demolished

It is true that three variant phrases all describe the assault of the flood waters:

                 18 intruding the might of rivers
                 24 the mouths together turned
                 25 against the wall directed the flow

But what these do is to divide the assault into three successive stages, spelling out details which are not repetitive of each other, but logically cumulative. As for the two concluding hexameters (32, 33), though they carry echoes of lines 19, 24 and 25, their vocabulary and syntax have been carefully manipulated so as to describe a reversal of previous action.

It is fair to conclude that the alphabetized Greek description of a flood is less tautological, less ritualized than the cuneiform. A vocabulary arrangement is applied to the task which is more expressive, as we would say, because it is richer in variety of nouns, verbs and adjectives, and less given to repetitive syntax, that is, to variations of the same essential statements. Both versions are of orally composed speech and therefore formulaic and repetitive to a degree which is uncharacteristic of literate discourse. But admitting this, in the Greek version we are brought into more direct contact with the complexities of human descriptive speech at its most concrete level; the Babylonian version by contrast simplifies the report, reducing it to a kind of archetypal statement, what can be called an "authorized version".[4]

A critic schooled in the ways of literacy would trace the difference to two differing views of "poetics," to two different poetic conventions or "styles" which a given language chooses to adopt, and would use the repetitive character of the Babylonian as an excuse to assign to it qualities of solemnity, grandeur, spiritual simplicity and the like. But a quite different explanation is possible, one which relies on the phonetic superiority of the alphabet over the cuneiform. According to this view, the deficiencies of cuneiform as an instrument of acoustic-visual recognition have discouraged the composer from packing into his verse the full variety of expression which such a description calls for: the alphabet on the other hand applied to a transcription of the same experience places no obstacles in the way of its complete phonetic translation.

If this is true, a further conclusion probably follows: the ability to describe the human experience fully in adequate language was surely available to the citizens of all urbanized cultures of the Near East, no less than to the Greeks. This capacity however was expressible orally and would not be available to writers. We must presume therefore that behind the scribal version of the flood which is all we have lies hidden forever, and lost to us forever, a far richer epic, linguistically speaking, or series of epics, which, obeying the law of cultural storage, performed for those cultures the functions that Homer performed for pre-literate Greece. This would be the poetry of the people, on their lips, in their memories, composed by Mesopotamian bards using formulaic rhythms comparable with the Greek, though as we have pointed out probably less sophisticated. What we have in cuneiform is not their words as they were spoken, but epitomes transcribed for recital on formal occasions, even though the Gilgamesh epic is classified by scholars as a secular poem.

The limits of expressive speech which impose themselves upon the Gilgamesh poem are shared by the entire "literature" so called of the Near East. If we may quote from an authoritative judgment: "The first shortcoming in texts from Mesopotamia is the consistent absence of any expression of that civilizations's uniqueness in the face of an alien background. . . . The second and closely related negative characteristic is the absence of any polemic in cuneiform literature. There is no arguing against opposing views; we find here none of the revealing dialogue which in Greek life and thought finds expression in court, in the theater, and in the lecture room. This might well be the main reason why we know so little about Mesopotamian attitudes towards the *realities of the world around them* (my italics) and so much about the Greek . . . No effort is made to relate within one conceptual framework differences in outlook or evaluation. Hence, all cuneiform texts have to be carefully interpreted with these *curiously inhibiting* and ultimately falsifying constraints in mind." [5]

What might the Greek account of the Homeric flood have become if committed to a syllabary instead of an alphabet? Obviously we have no means of knowing; it is impossible for us to recreate the mental processes of a Mesopotamian scribe or a Mycenaean one. If Linear B had survived to be used for Homer, one can only suggest some ways in which this might have been done. A narrative too rich for the script could be brought under control by a simplification of vocabulary and syntax while retaining the essentials. A transcription of the first four lines of our passage might offer few difficulties of recognition, for the sequence runs easily and the mind of the decipherer would readily make out the correct acoustic guesses. The catalogue might have the formulaic ring of an accepted list. A shorthand version however might be tempted to sacrifice the sense of line 19 since no loss of essentials is involved, and would certainly be tempted to omit lines 22 and 23 which interrupt the description by a new thought which momentarily transfers mental attention elsewhere. The senses of lines 26, 32 and 33 would likewise be expendable. The motive for such omissions would be to reduce the effort of recognizing not only new words but new arrangements of words and it would be no less powerful for being unconscious. Such suggestions are offered only by way of speculation, but the fact that simplification of discourse when transcribed in pre-alphabetic systems did occur is not in itself a speculative matter.

So we return to that unique paradox: an alphabetized Homer. By applying a new technology of the written word, there is made available in documented form the first complete report of an undocumented culture, not only the first of its kind, but for all time unique, for some infection of literacy has since invaded all oral cultures wherever experienced, robbing the investigator of that complete confrontation with total orality provided by the Homeric text.

The primary advantage offered by the alphabet over previous writing systems was to provide the power to document the oral report fluently and exhaustively. The language of the two poems is as compendious as their content. As the narrative proceeds, the *nomos* and *ethos* of a whole society are acted out. The nearest analogue in this respect would lie not in the surviving pockets of oral poetry practiced on the fringes of literate bureaucracies, as for example in the Balkans, in Russia, in Finland. For this kind of poetry does not carry encyclopedic responsibilities. The analogues would lie if anywhere in the epics recoverable from African or Polynesian societies if uncontaminated by documentation. Yet the analogues are necessarily imperfect; the societies which have yielded such pure specimens of orality appear to be relatively simple in structure compared with the Greek and thus the requirements placed on storage are correspondingly simple. If the range of human experience, the variety of human dilemmas that require directive help within family and village are less complex, the epic which supplies the directives will itself be less complex. Furthermore the transcription of this orality is conducted under different terms. In the Greek case the users of the language were themselves the discoverers of the new craft of transcription and applied it directly to what they themselves were saying without help of any foreign intermediary. Continuous oral recital of contrived speech and continuous transcription of such speech proceeded side by side for a long time within the same community; but for African and Polynesian cultures the alien anthropologist has to learn a language not his own before transcribing its sounds into a sign system which is not theirs. He cannot match and mate sign and sound with the same immediate and instinctive intimacy that the first Greeks employed. Lastly, as a translator, he will employ the idiom of his own speech, thus repeating and importing 2,500 years of literate development of the human consciousness, which comes between himself and the speech that he is translating.

The "moments" of mimesis

The conditions in oral society under which the Homeric poems came into existence make it impossible for the critic to distinguish between creative composition and mechanical repetition, as though these represented two categories mutually exclusive, the first of which was superseded by the second. To make the distinction, as is commonly done, is to rely on canons of judgment drawn from our experience of literature as a literate phenomenon. At all stages of the Homeric process, now lost in the mists of anonymity, we should speak only in hyphenated terms of the composer-reciter, the singer-rhapsode. Whether in individual instances the powers he commanded amounted to genius or merely skill, they consisted in the manipulation of two kinds of spell, or rather of one single spell directed in two different directions, one upon himself and his mouth, the other upon his audience and their ears. In both cases the spell was urgently required by the need to memorize verbal statements arranged in a fixed repeatable order, these extending in length from the formulas composing the parts of the hexameter, to the moral formulas incorporated in narrative situations, to the situations themselves, and to those series of situations which make up an episode, and to a given number of episodes which compose a total narration.

The mental effort required is difficult for the literate mind wholly to imagine, but it obviously meant a total absorption, a mental immersion in the act of recital. Plato described it by the term *mimesis*, which in this context comes close to meaning the "miming" of a mythos, its acting out by sympathetic identification with the characters and actions described.[6] The singer responding to a prompt in his mind—or one supplied by his audience—will proceed to tell us about Patroclus and Achilles, let us say, how Patroclus fought and fell in Achilles' place. He commits himself to recollecting the start of a given sound sequence leading into the mythos, and to a parallel recollection of what that mythos was all about. It was not indeterminate; it had its beginning, middle and end, which he is aware of as he begins the recital and which becomes more definite in realization as he proceeds, first to himself, and then to his audience who follow his song murmuring it to themselves. A modern audience at a musical recital likes to demonstrate its sophistication by preserving immobility as the strains reach their ears; no such intellectualized isolation was ever possible for the members of a culture of oral communication and oral memorization.

Such absorption controlled by rhythm of words, of instruments, and of body, meant that in the period of a given recitation the reciter remained totally indifferent to the existence of all mythoi other than the one that he happened to be reciting. He cannot think of them or relate to them unless and until the mythos he is committed to has been completed as a movement. Then and only then might his memory call up from its reserves a second one with linkage to the first. His rhythmic recollection proceeds by elocutions which are performed in intense self-absorbed moments of activity. Memory varies according to individual capacity. Singers therefore varied in their capacity to hold a single mythos without faltering and in their capacity to command a repertoire of such.

The sophistication of the verse technique, no less than the life style of the participants in the stories, argue for a period of oral composition which matured with the maturation of the Greek city state in Ionia. Homer's is not peasant poetry. For a century or more before the process of transcription began, a group of bards, or two groups, let us say, had become specialists not only in the Trojan War story but in two applications of the story known as the *Wrath* and the *Return*. Possibly some of them individually commanded the art of reciting all the parts, the individual mythoi which came to make up the *Iliad* and the *Odyssey* in our texts. This we shall never know. But a knowledge of the overall scene, the general *context*—(which is a literate term), or the "ideal epic" as some critics have called it,[7] was shared by all of them. An individual singer could break in on the overall scene when he pleased, without being aware of its sequence precisely as that is required in our present texts. Parts of what to us is a required sequential whole could be recited backwards from our standpoint, or told in what we with our fixed texts before us would call a string of *selections* (another literate term, as though speech consisted of alphabetized pieces to be picked up). A poet could switch attention to another mythos or piece of the epic—how many such pieces he might command would depend on his individual capacity—he would have to recall how to begin it and as he did so he would recall his prompting lines. But as he proceeded he would temporarily forget what he had just been saying as he continuously exchanged one set of absorptions for another, replacing one moment of memory by another.

In sum, the acoustic memory is associative but not comprehensive; it lives and works by temporary total commitment to a stretch of mythos before passing in transition to a different mythos constituting a fresh act of recollection. But the second will still share the same ethos as the first, for both in their expression must reflect and preserve the mores of the culture; both are parts of the same cultural encyclopedia, so that, digression and repetition aside, and allowing for some inevitable inconsistencies, style and substance remain uniform to a degree beyond anything that a "committee" of literate poets could manage.

It is to be concluded that our *Iliad* and *Odyssey* were recited sporadically in self-contained performances of individual episodes.[8] We cannot now disentangle what these were; the documentary organization later applied was extraordinarily skillful. Adopting the divisions of the text as we now have it, any attempt to imagine what these recitals might have been is tempted to envisage them as governed by the presents division into 24 books. We can only say that such a division represents the decisions made by the literate eye of later scholarship. In spirit, this was carried out in some sympathy with the original genius of oral performance—that is, episodes in the canonical text are separated from each other by natural breaks in most cases. There is no reason to suppose that this corresponds with fidelity to the original recitation process. We are asking in effect what were the separate pieces of each poem which after documentation were brought in all probability together in Athens, and arranged in the sequence we now have. We shall never know, though it is a little easier to guess what they may have been in the case of the *Odyssey*. The journey and return of Telemachus, for example, and the voyages narrated by Odysseus could be recited as self-contained mythoi in whole or in parts. To make some guesses about the *Iliad* is more difficult because its present arrangement is more intricate. In a very few cases a whole book or major part thereof stands out as a self-contained mythos. This is true of the twenty-fourth (the ransoming of Hector), and of the twenty-third, from line 259 (the funeral games), or of the tenth (an epic of night operations), or of the second, from line 87 to line 483 (the panic and rallying of the Greek army after nine years of war). A single recitation, of course, need not be confined to the length represented by a single book. There are a few sequences of books which could make up a recitation as they stand; 16 with 17 narrate the career and death of Patroclus; 8 and 9 describe the Trojan advance, the Greek retreat, and the Greek appeal to Achilles for rescue. More intricately, one can become aware of books now separated in our text which in continuity could have been recited as single thematic sequences. Thus Book One which describes the failure to resolve a quarrel with fatal effects predicted for the Greeks could be followed by Book Eight in which these effects occur and then by Book Nine where a second attempt is made to remedy the situation. The names of Achilles, Agamemnon, Nestor and Odysseus and their words and deeds dominate both Books One and Nine. Still more intricately, what would now be viewed as selections in our text could have been part of whole recitations now redistributed. This could be true, for example, of the domestic comedy acted out on Olympus, now distributed throughout the poem. The divine family presided over by its autocrat is presented in Book One, 493 to the end; later we see Hera and Athene descending from Olympus to interfere and then returning (5.711 to the end), whereat Zeus orders his household to maintain neutrality and then withdraws to Mount Ida (8.1–52), only to be seduced there by Hera (14.153–353), so that the family on Olympus can abandon neutrality while he sleeps, until he awakes in anger and despatches the orders which compel his willful household to restore the status quo (15.4–235). Such a combination would produce a single memorizable recitation of a mythos about the gods sung in a consistent key of comic realism.

Such are offered as examples, wholly hypothetical, of the kinds of recitations which lie below the continuities that we now call the *Iliad* and the *Odyssey*. The poems as we have them offer too many possibilities of permutation and combination for us to accept any one proposed arrangement as authentically original. Any one portion sung singly contains allusion in which the mythos of the whole epic is implicit. The reciter is aware of the existence of this ideal epic, it is present by implication. But the singer's attention is fastened upon his immediate theme; his memory is temporarily steeped in it to the exclusion of other considerations.

The echo-principle

Within this psychological commitment to rhythm and to the flow of rhythmic speech it is possible to determine an acoustic law at work which serves to supply connection as a kind of binding principle which ties bundles of recited situations together. It can be called the principle of the echo sounding in the ear with which is combined the principle of the mirror reflection presenting itself to the mind's eye. The first book of the *Iliad* provides a simple illustration: there at the beginning of the story is the priest on the seashore addressing Apollo with complaints; we wait awhile and the story proceeds and there is Achilles on the seashore addressing his mother with complaints. The formulas used in the first instance are repeated with necessary variation for the second and a physical scene once used is reflected in its counterpart. The principle can extend itself to include larger complexes of actions and situations. Thus in Book One the narrative relates how the *agora* met, how Nestor with suitable exhortation tries to mediate the quarrel, how Agamemnon despatches two emissaries to Achilles to take away Briseis. In Book Nine the mythos has moved on but the echo returns. The reciter narrates how the *agora* meets again, is superseded by a council in which Nestor with appropriate exhoratation once more mediates, and how Agamemnon dispatches emissaries to Achilles to restore Briseis. The echo principle is operative even to the point of re-using for three persons in the second instance the formulas which were appropriate for two persons in the first. This kind of mechanism is directly acoustic and only indirectly imagist. It is persistent in both poems and has been well documented by Homeric scholars, but with this difference, that the mechanism is interpreted in visual terms alone and is described as a pattern rather than as an echo, as though panels of matching series were arranged in sequences like aba, abba, abcba, and the like in the manner of painted altar-pieces.[9] But it was the ear, not the eye, that had to be seduced and led on by such arrangements, relying on the actual sounds of identical or similar words enclosed in similar sounding formulas and paragraphs.

Echo is something that the ear of singer and audience is trained to wait for. Its mnemonic usefulness encourages the presence of anticipation. We can say of the second instance that it echoes the first or of the first that it prophesies the second. Oral mythos is continually stretched forward in this way as it is told in order to assist recall in the reciter's mind of how the mythos is to proceed, what the plot is to be. Echo, however, is modified. It is not a duplicate, for a duplicate would say nothing more than had already been said; the tale would degenerate into mindless repetition. The echo must accompany a fresh statement of fresh action, but this cannot be excessively novel or inventive; to accommodate the needs of memory there must be enough likeness to the prior statement to seduce or tempt the mind to make the leap from one to the other, and to tempt the mouth to follow with the appropriate enunciation. The constant need for a mechanism of anticipation and confirmation explains the prominence in oral epic poetry, among other things, of prophesy and prophetic statements put into the mouths of characters even in the moment of an action which they perform in the present. Achilles warns Patroclus not to go too far—so we anticipate that he will and maybe dangerously so; Apollo protests to the gods in council that Achilles' maltreatment of Hector must stop—so we know it is going to stop; Calchas must speak but he is afraid of offending somebody powerful—so we are warned that offense will be given and that a bitter feud is likely to follow.

Spoken language is a continuum, a soundtrack manufactured by the larynx and carried on waves in the air, divisible acoustically into moments but not spatially into extended panels. Moments which anticipate and echo each other are con-sonant, not symmetrical. An episode describing martial combat is filled with language noises which recall or are associated with fighting; a banquet scene with words of eating, drinking and merrymaking. Telemachus' journey in the Peloponnese is carried forward in repeated locutions which describe horses and chariots running, harness jingling as it is put on and taken off, cups of hospitality filled and drunk and emptied, greetings given and received. In the *Iliad*, a quarrel between two men is conducted in a series of responsions with similar epithets of hostility exchanged. There is a high element of onomatopoeia in orally memorized composition.

Such are the mnemonic mechanisms which control and guide the incantation of the verse and impose the necessary spell upon the consciousness of singer and audience. If we have dwelt on them in this place, it is to reinforce the conclusion earlier stated that oral composition and recitation both proceed in moments of intense activity, the moment being understood as a self-contained movement within a given mythos, during the performance of which the memory of other episodes is suspended. The reciter is absorbed in his present context and moves through it from beginning to conclusion in total indifference to other contexts outside the period that he is accomplishing.

The journey and the dream

Proto-literate Greece after Homer, at a time when the concepts of intellectual activity and the procedures of discursive thought were surfacing in the consciousness, found some difficulty in verbalizing them, in defining or describing the cognitive process. One word adopted to describe it was *hodos*, a journeying down a way, an itinerary; the word symbolizes both the route and the taking of the route. The philosopher Parmenides resorts to this metaphor and Plato revives it. As a piece of terminology it lives in the no-man's land between non-literate and literate habit; it catches the sense of the oral connective process and it is significant that both thinkers suggest that this route within the mind can be circular. It catches the sense of the oral reciter's commitment to a track of sound and speech which he follows rather than one which he himself directs. He is still the traveler with his feet moving along the road absorbed in marking the direction set for him, watching the signs set by the roadside; not the intellectual who calculates the steps that he is to take successively one by one in full consciousness. Often he will return on his tracks: "it is all one to me where I begin," says Parmenides, faithfully reproducing the plunge that the bard takes into a medium from which he also emerges having told his tale.

Another metaphor applied by Plato to the psychological situation of the poet and the audience is that of the dream from which both of them, bewitched by the images which pass before them, like sleepwalkers have to be awakened before they can become aware of "what is." [10] Platonism sets its foundations upon this awakened state of consciousness and calls the condition which precedes it by the Greek term *doxa*, which is not very happily translated as "opinion." One can appreciate the relevance of the dream-metaphor to the absorption of the oral poet both in composition and in performance (*mimesis*), bearing in mind that composition is itself an act of memory while performance is the act that seeks to imprint that memory on others. The dream is something which takes charge of us rather than vice versa. We surrender to it and our surrender while temporary is total in the sense that any connection with other mental states is broken, whether these are other dreams or the wakened state of controlled consciousness identifiable with intellection. An overall context of "meaning," or relevance to experience in general, is absent. Only by a restructuring of the language that one is using can one seek to establish such a context and this means a restructuring of one's psychology. The dream is equivalent to the moment of rhapsodic recitation.

The "dating" of "Homer"

The literate historian of archaic Greece just because he is literate when he approaches the problem of when and how Homer was written down is prone to visualize this as a single event; to postulate that the technology of the alphabet once invented would be applied wholesale to the transcription of a work previously existing in oral form; rather as a writer today commits his composition to paper and the typed paper is then transmitted to the printer to emerge from the press as a completed volume. Just so, the Greek "writer," whether visualized as rhapsodist or as scribe, is imagined to seat himself at a desk (tablets in his lap would not suffice) in order to transcribe on to rolls of papyrus (perhaps sheets of vellum, though this is unlikely) the *Iliad* and the *Odyssey* respectively.

This is an improbable picture; the invention of the alphabetic sign-code, by adding vocalics to the Phoenician series, was one thing. Its fluent application to the transcription of language in quantity was quite another. Writing on this scale would presume a habit developed into an art. We should rather ask: given the fact that the epic enjoyed a purely auditory existence, memorized and repeated orally, what was likely to be the original motive for bringing this contrived language into contact with the signs of the alphabet? The probable answer is one that is supplied in later notices in Pindar and Aeschylus:[11] it is also one that grows out of the oral operation itself. The motive was mnemonic, a response to the same psychological pressures that had inspired and governed the oral technique; the alphabetic signs offered a supplement to the energies required for memorization.

How was this to be done with a technique still in its infancy so far as fluent application is concerned? Surely by transcribing bits and pieces of the oral verse, such bits and pieces being used as prompters to remind a reciter how to start, or for that matter how to stop. They might perhaps grow into little epitomes of episodes which the reciter otherwise held in his head as his preferred repertoire. Gradually, and with recognition of the reduced effort required if they could be re-read, such transcriptions would extend themselves to the recording of whole portions of the verse. As a hypothetical illustration of this practice: the introductory lines to the *Iliad* could conveniently become a written piece, for they predict the course of the plot—prediction being the method of oral mnemonic—and so the bard might welcome the chance to read it over to remind him of the chief elements of his story before he launches into it. The catalogue in the second book was surely one of the earliest portions committed to writing. The two councils of the gods in the *Odyssey* which successively set portions of the action moving might be another example which if transcribed would be especially convenient. Details of this sort we shall never know but the hypothesis of partial transcription of "reminders," constituting the original use to which the alphabet was put, is surely not fanciful.

This amounts to saying that alphabetization was originally a function of oral recitation; the two were intermingled. If so, in order to understand the circumstances under which alphabetization was completed, we should consider the likely conditions of oral performance during the period when, according to our hypothesis, Homer was being partially and imperfectly alphabetized. The earliest inscriptions—a small group—cluster round the date 700 B.C. They are metrical, and widely dispersed.[12] On the other hand, the first lyric verse which we may be sure was actually transcribed in the lifetime of its author, by himself or through his dictation, was composed by Archilochus of Paros in the mid-seventh century. This perhaps is an over-cautious inference based on the extreme scantiness both of the remains of earlier poets and of the tradition surrounding their names. Is it possible that portions of the *Iliad* and *Odyssey* were transcribed not earlier than were the poems of Archilochus? We shall never of course know the precise answer but the question is not out of order. As for the terminus ante quem, the point at which we can assume either the *Iliad* or the *Odyssey* achieved that complete textual existence with which we are familiar, the tradition, already current before the end of the fifth century, [13] which stated that the Homeric poems were put in order after some fashion in Athens during the reign of Pisistratus or his sons, need not be disputed. [14] The alphabetization of Homer in the sense in which we know Homer might have been completed as late as 520 B.C., or earlier. So far as this tradition has been rejected, this has been due more than anything else to the presumption that Greece was fully literate at least as early as 700 B.C. and perhaps earlier, in which case the poems were likely to have been both written and read in what we call their cononical form much earlier than the reign of Pisistratus. But the presumption that Greece was fully literate before 500 B.C. (or indeed before 430 B.C.) would appear to be unfounded. [15]

The act of visual integration

As documentation takes place, a restless, moving sea of words becomes frozen into immobility. Each self-contained moment of recitation—an episode or a set of such—becomes imprisoned in an order no longer acoustic but visible. It ceases to be a soundtrack and becomes almost a tangible object. A collocation of such objects takes place as they are gathered and written. Because they are now preserved outside the individual memories of those who inscribe and gather them, the gatherer need no longer surrender himself totally and temporarily to absorption in any one of them. He is able to look at them in the mass and become aware of them as a sum, a totality. As he does this he begins to wake up from the dream. His relaxed consciousness allows his eye, not his ear, to rove at will over the sum total and as he does so he will begin to compare the parts with each other visually. Part of the attention previously concentrated on the recitation of any one of them becomes directed to a visual comtemplation of the whole.

An individual oral recitation, being a mythos, tells a tale in temporal sequence without flashback or major digression. But once the mythoi are *seen* together, it will be perceived that recitation A, describing the story of Odysseus' adventures, let us say, during his wanderings, and recitation B, the story of his detention by the nymph Calypso, his escape and shipwreck, and recitation C, the story of Telemachus going in search of his father, all deal with time periods which overlap with each other. Or let us say that the story of how the Greeks grew demoralized after nine years of war and broke ranks and then rallied and resumed the offensive needs to be related in time to the story of how Achilles and Agamemnon quarreled and how this brought about a Trojan offensive; and yet again to the story of Achilles' onslaught on the Trojans and how he routed them en masse and killed Hector. It naturally occurred to the reflective eye that the principle of temporal sequence which had been applied in individual recitations should be applied if possible to the whole mass. How place the pieces in a similar sequence? It cannot be done, very simply because these original recitations recited separate events many of which when viewed together can be seen to take place within overlapping time-spans. Moreover, in addition to the echo principle employed within each one, all recitations contain predictions or allusive statements which refer in passing to what is going to happen to a character or has already happened to him outside the context of a given recitation. These constitute fleeting memories of the fact that there is an ideal epic larger than any one single recitation. So a compromise is struck. The story pieces are sorted out and numbered so as to achieve the effect of a single overall time sequence which moves forward but with interruptions, flashbacks, and digressions to an appointed end. Thus arose the arrangement of our present text, correctly designated by Homeric critics as an *ordo artificialis*,[16] this *ordo* being the work of the eye not the ear, a work achievable only when the various portions of the soundtrack had been alphabetized.

It is at this point when visual organization is superimposed upon an acoustic one that an architecture of language becomes conceivable within which the phonetic principles of connection are accommodated. All the literate and the literary terminology now commonly applied to organized discourse begins to come into its own. The author of any preserved discourse becomes not just a singer but a "composer," his product becomes a "work" possessing "pattern" and "structure," controlled by "theme," "topic," or "subject." Even his actors become "characters." His activity in the case of the Homeric poems becomes "monumental."[17] These and dozens of other terms are drawn from the visual, tactile experience of handling alphabetized script. They lie outside the thought world of an oral culture and of the singers who originally sang the songs that we call Homeric. Henceforth it becomes possible that a Greek "literature" in the literate sense should come into being.

But it is to be stressed that the essence of language as a phonetic system could not be transcended and is not wholly transcended to this day. The works of Greek literature after the Homeric transcription occurred are composed in an increasing tension between the genius of oral and the genius of written composition. Because orality remained so close to the Greeks to the end of the fifth century, and indeed continuing into the fourth, the degree of this tension was unique in the literature of the period. Athenian drama, in addition to being rhythmic, obeys the associative and predictive rules of oral composition; it is composed on the echo principle and is conceived as a performance to be heard and seen and memorized but not to be read. It is also composed as a cultural record, an Athenian supplement to the Homeric encyclopedia. Yet it is very plain that it also employs the architecture of composition which only the writer's eye could supply. It represents an intermediate art retaining the specific energies latent in oral incantation, yet submitting to the reflective control exercised by a dawning intellectualism. As such, it could never be duplicated in any later culture unless our world were to collapse into total non-literacy and we all had to start again.

Documentation of discourse in Greece took time and originally was confined to inscribing what had previously been composed metrically according to oral rules. The invention of a prose which would realize the full potential of the word inscribed, the scope of expression available when the word no longer needed memorization to survive, took even longer. Its progress can be marked in the texts of Herodotus, Thucydides and Plato. The reasons for the delay lie in a law which is fundamental to the history of the human word: the modes of literate discourse whatever they may be cannot be understood apart from an understanding of the modes of non-literate discourse. Each is intimately bound up with the other, the oral because it would not exist for us without the literate resources; the literate because the sophistication of its own vocabulary and syntax grew out of changes and transpositions in the oral vocabulary and syntax and cannot properly be understood without grasping what these changes were. The very task which literate communication sets itself—the creation and the conservation of knowledge, technological and cultural—was first confronted and solved in the uncounted millennia of oral experience when man knew no knowledge other than that which was contained in the sounds of his language as they were pronounced.

NOTES AND REFERENCES

[1] Problems surrounding the transcription of oral poetry came to scholarly attention with the publication of A.B. Lord's *Singer of Tales* (Harvard 1960) caps. 6 and 7. Cf. also G.S. Kirk *Songs of Homer* (Cambridge 1962) cap. 14; A.M. Parry, "Have We Homer's *Iliad?*" YCS XX (1966). Preparation of the present article has rested upon argument supplied in some of my previous publications: *Preface to Plato* (Harvard 1963) chaps. 1–4; "Prologue to Greek Literacy" in *University of Cincinnati Classical Studies Semple Lectures* Vol. II (Oklahoma 1973; *Origins of Western Literacy: Ontario Institute for Studies in Education Monograph Series* /14 (1976; "The Preliteracy of the Greeks" in *New Literary History* (*University of Virginia*) Vol. VIII, no. 3 (1977). See also Robert Kellogg "Oral Literature" in *New Literary History* Vol. V no. 1 (1973). Two articles by J.A. Davison on "Literature and Literacy in Ancient Greece" (*Phoenix* Vol. XVI nos. 3 and 4 (1962) are also relevant, as is the same author's support, given in *A Companion to Homer* (Cambridge 1962), for authenticity of the tradition which placed some consolidation of the Homeric text in the age of Pisistratus.

[2] "Origins" (above note 1) pp. 22–50.

[3] *The Ancient Near East: An Anthology of Texts edited by James B. Pritchard* (Princeton 1958), pp. 68–9.

[4] "Origins" p. 34. G.K. Gresseth in "The Gilgamesh Epic and Homer" *C.J.* 70, no. 4 (1975) pp. 1–18, argues for closer stylistic congruence: the two "are cast in the same literary genre, the heroic epic" (p. 17).

[5] A. Leo Oppenheim, "The Position of the Intellectual in Mesopotamian Society," *Daedalus* Spring 1975 p. 38.

[6]*Preface* (above note 1) chap. 2.

[7]I borrow the phrase from Kellogg (above note 1) p. 59.

[8]The Homeric terms are *aoidē, oimē, muthos* and also *molpē* and *hymnos*. Frequent descriptions in both poems (especially *Odyssey*) of musical-poetic recitation allude always to performances of episodes.

[9]C.H. Whitman *Homer and Heroic Tradition* (Harvard 1958), chap. 5, stresses the parallel between Homeric patterning and geometric art.

[10]*Preface* pp. 190, 238 ff.

[11]Pindar *Ol.* 10.1 ff; Aesch. *Suppl.* 179. *Choeph.* 450, *Eum.* 275, *P.V.* 460, 789–90.

[12]Cf. "Preliteracy" (above note 1).

[13]It is probably alluded to in Isocrates' *Panegyricus* and reported in Plato's *Hipparchus* (a dialogue included in the ancient canon and accepted by many Platonic scholars). Though these works were composed early in the fourth century B.C. their authors were born in 436 and 429 respectively.

[14]Cf. Davison in *Companion* (above note 1).

[15]Cf. "Preliteracy" and *Preface* chap. 3.

[16]So Davison, in *Companion*.

[17]Kirk *Songs* (above note 1) p. 316 would assign "monumental composition" to oral poetry of the 8th century B.C.

KEVIN ROBB, a native of Southern California, was born in 1936. He was educated at Georgetown University and did his graduate work at Yale, where he took a Ph.D. in Classical Philosophy. He has held, among other scholarships, a Danforth Fellowship, a Leavey Fellowship, and was awarded a major research grant for the study of Greek epigraphy by the National Endowment for the Humanities. He has published widely in journals of classics, archeology and philosophy, and is the author of a number of articles in the most recent (1974) edition of the *Encyclopaedia Britannica*. A book on the complete Presocratic fragments (coauthored with Eric Havelock) is in preparation. He is at present Associate Professor of Philosophy at the University of Southern California. Previously he was Visiting Scholar at the University of Istanbul and also taught for the Bilingual Department of Humanities at the American College in Istanbul.

Poetic Sources of the Greek Alphabet: Rhythm and Abecedarium from Phoenician to Greek[*]

by KEVIN ROBB

O NE OF THE safer generalizations in the comparative history of cultures is that human beings are slow to realize the full potential of an innovation in their technology. Almost at random one thinks of the cultivation of grains, the internal combustion engine, moveable type, the computer, even the stirrup

* My debts in this paper are diverse and only partially acknowledged in it, but none equals that to Eric Havelock. Research was in part funded by a grant from the National Endowment for the Humanities which I acknowledge with gratitude.

and the movie camera. Technological innovations which one day will revolutionize societies or at least significantly alter life styles initially are called into existence only to accomplish some familiar task in a slightly better way. But gradually variations in the uses of the technology itself lead to bolder experiments until at last it is clear even to reluctant observers that exploding advances in a technology are changing not only the way people live, but how they speak and think. Such, I suggest, was in fact the case with a technological innovation which, more decisively than any other, was to affect the intellectual history of Western man, the Greek alphabet.

The remarkable character of the event was well stated some years ago by George Mylonas:

> Of the discoveries made by man in his long career in our planet, and they are many and awe-inspiring, few surpass in interest and in importance his invention of the art of writing. To be able by means of twenty-four or twenty-six characters to communicate to others our deepest thoughts, our strongest emotions, and our innermost desires, is an achievement that borders on the miraculous. Ages of effort lie behind this achievement . . . .[1]

However, the event itself, the creation of the first complete alphabet, and the conditions which must have given rise to it, have been little understood or even studied by scholars. To be sure, the date of the event was for a time controversial, but of late most scholars are not inclined seriously to dispute the conclusions of Rhys Carpenter; the consensus of current scholarship places the invention of the Greek alphabet not earlier than the middle of the eighth century.[2] The Phoenician rather than the Aramaic source for the actual letter forms has for even a longer time been beyond controversy. Since Sir Leonard Wolley's excavation of a Greek trading post on Phoenician territory at Al Mina, and now that Albright and others have demonstrated the extensive and early character of the Phoenician mercantile enterprise, various possible locations for the event have been plausibly advanced, none of course conclusively.[3] But actual site is perhaps unimportant as long as it can be demonstrated that a place with the requisite conditions was available. Old Phoenician was deciphered early in the last century and almost yearly more inscriptions are turning up. The limitations of this North Semitic vowelless script[4] compared to the flexibility of the Greek alphabet for recording the full range of human speech have been recognized and documented in the literature. But can we do no more?

For some time I have anticipated encountering an article in an archeological or classical journal disputing the common assumption that the Greeks borrowed their letters from the Phoenicians in order, like contemporary Phoenicians, to keep commercial accounts and to serve related mercantile needs. What troubled me is that precisely how Phoenician traders and ship captains kept their financial records ca. 700 B.C. is something which is completely unknown to us. If they were as wily as many of their present Lebanese descendants, then aging fathers may well have kept control of businesses away from sons (and tax collectors) by keeping the accounts totally in their heads. In any case, if there is no hard evidence for the mercantile uses of the script either among Greek or Phoenician ca. 700 B.C., then may we not speculate about the purposes for which the Greeks adopted the script, and what needs required them simultaneously to adapt it by providing signs for the vowels?

One defensible but neglected avenue of approach is to compare the earliest Greek inscriptions with their nearest Phoenician contemporaries and draw whatever conclusions the evidence indicates. The earliest Greek inscription is a graffito incised on the shoulder of the famous Dipylon oinochoe, consisting of one complete dactylic hexameter verse plus some readable letters of the beginning of a second verse.[5] The second hexameter trails upward toward the neck of the jug and the last letters reveal several false starts before the final scratching was done. The writer's hand, though firm, is unpracticed in the use of a script, but undeniably the writer himself is in complete possession of the already centuries-old technique of oral verse-making. This gulf between the poetic accomplishment of the line and the child-like hand which scratched it is initially the most striking feature of the Dipylon inscription, and perhaps an important clue. Could it be that the author was a wandering minstrel, an Homeric *aoidos*, who had only recently learned the Phoenician abecedarium in the form in which, within his own lifetime, these signs had been adapted for recording the sounds of Greek?

The completed hexameter, as transliterated and translated, reads:

ὃς νῦν ὀρχηστῶν πάντων ἀταλώτατα παίζει
Whoso of all the dancers now sports most playfully.

We cannot be certain of the second verse, but it probably would have read, "This jug as a prize is given," or the like. Clearly the wine jug was a prize in some Attic dance contest and seemingly the inscription records a previous oral pronouncement.

The dating of the inscription is no longer a matter of serious dispute among scholars.[6] This particular type of jug is assigned to near the end of the eighth century; probably it was fired in the last decades preceding the year 700 B.C. The graffito was scratched on the painted terracotta surface of the jug after it had been fired, but, given the cheapness of the ware, possibly not very long after. It is worth noting that although half a dozen other inscriptions date from the first quarter of the next century, none can with assurance be placed with the Dipylon in the eighth. Furthermore, all the alphas in the Dipylon inscription rest on their sides, a feature found in no other Attic inscription but a universal feature of the relevant Phoenician inscriptions. The direction of the writing is retrograde, as was all Phoenician writing prior to this time, and as it was to remain even after Greece had converted to boustrophedon and then to orthograde, the left-to-right direction. These are indications that the jug was incised near the period of the adoption of the North Semitic script, an event which now can probably be placed in the second half of the eighth century.

The next half century produced at most a dozen scraps of writing, and all of these, in so far as they are more than names, reveal the dominating influence of oral epic together with minor concessions to various local dialects. The number of inscriptions proliferates almost geometrically from ca. 650 onward, so that from the eighth century the progress of Greek literacy can be charted on an unbroken course in terms of an ever expanding body of surviving inscriptions.[7] How can the total silence before 750 B.C. be explained other than to conclude that the alphabet was invented around that date?

What deserves comment is that any survey of the earliest inscriptions reveals the following general features.[8] The surviving inscriptions are not mercantile; this includes the dedicatory inscriptions on the Perachora spits, the artifact alone being of an economic nature. All are metrical, and may betray in gradual eclipse the influence of oral epic, as indeed does the literature of the period and even such semi-official pronouncements as foundation oracles for new cities given by Delphi. Finally, and this is little noted, these early inscriptions are used for purposes remarkably similar to the contemporary Phoenician inscriptions, but with the difference that the Greek inscriptions have been adapted to the Greek cultural situation and traditional forms of expression. What we find from both Semite and Greek hands as they leave their similar marks on enduring substances are votive offerings and short commemorative notices on stone or on metal, vase markings, curse tablets, and later, in large numbers, funeral inscriptions. Written laws on stone or the like are in the Greek case fairly late in the story, and economic inscriptions much later still.

It is often assumed, as noted above, that the alphabet must have been borrowed by Greek merchants from Phoenician traders in order to help the Greek keep better accounts and commit to writing economic contracts and similar transitory mercantile items. Should we not rather ask under what conditions, and in response to what needs, the script might have been adopted and adapted in order to transfer Greek verse onto some enduring substance? The evidence clearly points in this direction as the actual motive for some itinerant eighth century Greek, possibly after visiting a Phoenician temple on Cyprus, to invent the Greek alphabet. A recently recovered Phoenician inscription from Spain dated by Semitic epigraphists to within decades of the Dipylon graffito is particularly instructive.

Published in 1966 by J.M. Solá-Solé and correctly dated to the eighth century, it consists of five lines of the Old Phoenician writing.[9] These lines are incised on a pedestal at the feet of a goddess; the bronze statuette with its inscribed pedestal was acquired by the Museo Arqueólogico de Sevilla in 1963. In a number of striking ways both statuette and inscription are reminiscent of the Mantiklos Apollo, a bronze statuette from Thebes dated to about 700 B.C.[10] Around the legs of this archaic statuette (more likely representing donor than god) is an inscription in the epic meter and language (with the normal slight intrusions of the local dialect) in which a certain Mantiklos appeals to Apollo the Far Darter for the god to grant him a favor. In the parallel Phoenician inscription a certain Ba'lyaton thanks Astart-Hor "our lady" for she heard and answered some petition. The nearly contemporary inscriptions with similar wording (both, within their respective traditions, are formulaic, betraying oral originals) in which replicas of divine or human figures in bronze are presented as thank offerings indicate a similar religious sentiment. Such a use of script must have been perceived as appropriate to the god and to human emotions and expectations.

Religious sentiments such as these, and the uses of writing involved in them, have of course persisted in the Aegean Basin to this day. In 1962 I visited a Greek church on Lindos at a site reportedly visited by St. Paul and there I saw illiterate Greek women offering before the icon of the Virgin candles to which were attached short written petitions. I discovered that the local priest was literate and would write the messages in return for a small offering. Later I discovered that the old woman in whose house I was staying avoided the offering by having one of my fellow boarders, a Canadian artist who spoke excellent Greek, write her messages to the Virgin for her.

The sentiment in these cases is possibly not so dissimilar from that behind the eighth century dedicatory inscriptions to Hurrian Astarte or Greek Apollo. The written message fixes the petition before the eyes of the god; the object speaks without ceasing as no mortal can, and writing personalizes the religious emotion, remaining as surrogate for the petitioner after she or he must depart back to daily tasks. The *grammata* or letters in the ancient phrase are "the remedies against oblivion." Something personal of oneself survives and the petition (or curse or lament) persists in writing as it never could in the ephemeral spoken word. We recognize this ourselves with our tradition of inscribed grave markers in granite, or even when we imbed a lover's initials linked to our own on a tree trunk.

Was the idea of a dedicatory inscribed statuette borrowed by Greeks by stimulus diffusion from the earlier Phoenician practice? There are two significant differences between the Greek and the Semitic cases and perhaps they are important clues to the sources of Greek literacy and the origins of the Greek alphabet itself. In the Greek inscriptions, and only in them, a fully developed system of vowel indication is present from the beginning. And moreover these inscriptions reflect the pervasive influence of oral epic. It is not likely to be the case that these two outstanding features in the relevant inscriptions are unrelated. Let us pursue the theory that they are closely connected by attempting to recreate the conditions under which the adaptation of the Phoenician abecedarium to suit the Greek cultural conditions may have taken place.

At once we must assume a community of bilinguals on friendly terms in a situation of established oral exchange and instruction. The flourishing bilingual centers of the eighth century on Cyprus, where Greek and Phoenician are brought together by the imperative need for metals,[11] are the likely candidates. At Kourion, or at Citium where recently in an eighth century Phoenician temple a new dedicatory inscription has been found, the Greek must have been able to observe the Phoenician doing something (e.g., possibly inscribing a votive statuette) which the Greek, by reason of a lacuna in his technology, could not do.[12] He not only must be able to observe the Phoenician; he must wish to imitate, and he must receive oral instruction. No amount of staring at a silent inscription could inform a Greek of the pronunciation of Phoenician weak consonants such that he could deduce that at least three of them suggest the pronunciation of the Greek vowels. No amount of silent contemplation could give to Greeks the order of the letters in the abecedarium, or the Semitic names which, on the acrophonic principle (*alep* = a, *bet* = b, *gimel* = g, *dalet* = d, etc.) yielded the pronunciation demanded by the signs.

However, when the Greek seeks to translate into his cultural situation what the Semite had for some time accomplished by means of a script in his, he turns unavoidably to epical speech, the meter and language of "Homer." Only this takes the occasion of the moment out of the ordinary and mundane and elevates it into a special enclave of language which evokes epic action, significance and promise of endurance. Sir Maurice Bowra has called attention to the Greeks' subjection to "the dominating Homeric presence" in the Archaic period.

> On the one hand they could not escape from it; its metre, its manner, much of its temper, and many of its devices were bred into their consciousness and indispensable to them. They could make innovations and variations and approach new subjects, but they still remained in thrall . . . We may conclude that, when in the latter part of the eighth century, men wished to speak about their present occasions or feelings, they resorted for aid to the language of the epic, that is of the whole oral tradition spread through many parts of Greece.[13]

This would explain the first outstanding feature of the early Greek inscriptions, namely their metrical character. The Semitic models were themselves not mercantile but literary. By stimulus diffusion the Greek resorted to epic verse to imitate what the Phoenician had accomplished within his own linguistic tradition. What then of the second striking feature? All of the vowels are noted by their separate signs wherever we would expect them; the same "weak" consonants have been converted to signs for the respective Greek vowels. The practice is invariable; it is found from the beginning in all Greek inscriptions.

One scholar (Larfeld) was sufficiently impressed by this fact that he suggested that only an edict from Delphi could have secured such wide and consistent compliance. More recently Ignace Gelb, a Semitic epigraphist, was willing to postulate a period of transitional inscriptions which would reveal the slow adaptation of the Semitic signs to designate the vowels. In the absence of evidence bearing witness to such a developmental period Professor Gelb remarks that nothing would surprise him less than if such a transitional inscription should turn up.[14] I will readily concede that the Greek achievement, the completion of the developmental history of writing by creating the world's first true alphabet, is impressive. However, I do not think we have to go to such extreme lengths to explain it. We need only reflect a moment on the nature of Greek epic verse, and on certain linguistic and metrical features which distinguish it from Semitic parallels.

Greek poetry, unlike much of Semitic, is metered; that is, the rhythm is created by a pattern of syllables which, by precise rules, are either long or short. It is a quantitative rather than, as in English poetry, a stressed rhythm. The value of the syllable as long or short is a function of the sequence of the vowels, taken either in themselves or in relationship to the consonants. Thus, when a Greek minstrel was in apprenticeship to a master-singer in the oral period, what his ear had to hear so precisely was the sequence of the vowels. These are of course the linguistic items which, within the Semitic language group, a written record, or a script, can most easily afford to ignore.

The poetic unit in Greek epic meter is the dactyl, which is constituted by a long syllable followed by two short syllables (-uu). The hexametric line of course is constituted by six such units. By a convention which may go back to Mycenaean times, a long is considered as equal to two shorts, so that a spondee (--) can ordinarily be substituted for a dactyl.

It follows that any Greek word containing three shorts in sequence (uuu), of which there are a good many, can never appear in a hexameter, and are, therefore, excluded from a singer's repertoire. Excluded too, are words which scan u-u or -u- unless the singer, being as ever acutely conscious of the *vowel* sounds, chooses artificially to lengthen one of them. Such rules are not whimsical. The reason for such restrictions is that the metrical frame is of *fixed* time length and does not permit a random multiplication of syllables without promptly destroying the singer's instrument and, therefore, his oral performance. The established time length is six feet and a foot is determined by the number of syllables it contains and whether they are long or short.

At root then Greek meter is a function of the sequence of consonant and vowel, so that it is the value of the *vowel*, in itself and in relationship to a consonant, which determines whether a syllable is long or short. It follows that the one thing to which an adequate written record of such a line could never be indifferent is the sequence of the vowels.

Let us now contrast this with the Semitic tradition. What is characteristic of the Semitic language group is, of course, that the consonantal root, normally three consonants such as *ktb*, persists and the internal vowels vary in order to express the syntactic function of the word in the sentence. Moreover, before the invention of the Greek alphabet and of the post-alphabetic diacritic system, only the consonants were written. The eye of the reader isolated the consonantal roots, and from the context, he, *the reader*, supplied the appropriate vowels. Rarely (but apparently as early as the Ugaritic texts) a weak consonant could be added to a consonantal cluster in order to specify the pronunciation of a terminal vowel (hence the name *matres lectionis*, or mothers of reading) but this was a sporadic device and did not effect a transition from what structurally remained the Semitic unvocalized syllabaries to complete alphabets.

However, such scripts are less inadequate for preserving Semitic poetry than they would be for preserving Greek verse. The reason is that the rhythm is provided by different devices in the different traditions. In the Greek tradition the rhythm is set up by a pattern of long and short syllables; in the Semitic it is normally provided by parallelism or a balancing of members, whether of expressions or ideas or both. Some examples will readily make this clear.

The twenty-eighth chapter of Deuteronomy seeks to enjoin compliance to a behavior code by promising blessings or curses on the heads of those who, respectively, do or do not comply. The curses alone occupy some fifty-four verses, and in the learned estimate of Delbet Hillers, could be intoned in about twelve minutes, "an achievement in non-stop malediction which would have excited the admiration of Mark Twain."[15] I give a short selection in Hillers' translation.

> You will be cursed in the city, and cursed in the country . . . cursed when you come in, and cursed when you go out . . . And the sky o'er your head shall be copper, and the ground beneath you, iron.

These particular curses[16] betray composition by rhythmic parallelism and, in my judgment, betray behind the written version a grim oral mnemonic. The principle, as in all rhythm is the echo, or "lead on." The mind is aided in the act of recall by the fact that something in the first member of a balanced pair suggests, or leads the memory on, to something parallel (or opposite) in the second member. Much of the "prose" of Heraclitus, for instance, which is the earliest Greek literary prose extant, is composed on this principle, and betrays by its stylistic features that the Heraclitean *logoi* were framed to be carried in the hearer's memory. In the present case, to think of the city is to suggest its opposite, the country; to come in suggests to go out; sky over head suggests land under feet, and each, in turn, is associated with an appropriate metal, copper and iron. Similar mnemonic needs dictated that all early preserved oral communication of any length by rhythmed, the Semitic tradition in general emphasizing a balance of members, the Greek tradition in general emphazing meter. However, only in the Greek metrical tradition is the notation of the sequence of the vowels crucial once the poetic unit is committed to writing.

A second example is provided by the decipherment of Ugaritic, an accomplishment which at once revealed its affinities to Hebrew and Phoenician. A Ugaritic poetic unit reads: "Dew of heavens; fat of earth." A Hebrew version reads: "From the dew of the heavens and the fat of the earth."[17] Both probably derive from a common oral prototype framed to meet mnemonic needs. In any case, the consonantal skeleton is the same in both versions for the words translated "dew," "heavens," "fat" and "earth." What analysis discovers is a poetry created by a parallelism of balanced members, and therefore a rhythm of "lead on." The dew (a demonstration or product of fertility) of heavens suggests fat (similarly a product of fertility or prosperity) of earth, which in turn is the opposite of heavens. The mind in expressing one member is automatically helped, or lead on, to the other. The language in such cases may not be technically metered, but it remains poetic, with the solemnity and dignity such traditional phrasing betrays either to ear or eye.

Now let us turn to the situation of bilingual instruction between Phoenician and Greek. The Phoenician explains to his Greek counterpart the function of his votive inscription (or curse tablet or whatever artifact it is they have before them) as he also explains what writing is capable of accomplishing in his culture. The Greek detects at once what we who study the body of Phoenician inscriptions also realize: this is not the trivial discourse of the market place, the shop talk of traders. The formulae and repetitions and balanced clauses, the poetry of rhythmed members, the product of a long Semitic oral tradition, suggests a dignity and solemn significance which only the rigidly metered speech of epic conveys in the Hellenic tradition. Simultaneously, if the art of writing is here being transferred, we must also imagine the sequence of the letters, and their pronunciation, being orally communicated.

What would have struck the Greek as inadequate in the Semitic abecedarium as he hears it rehearsed by the instructing Phoenician, (and as the Greek thinks ahead to transferring an epic verse onto a votive offering to Apollo or Aphrodite), is that the abecedarium makes no provision for noting in the medium of the eye what the Greek's ear must hear so acutely, the sequence of the vowels. But suppose also that certain of the Phoenician letters, the weak consonants, are superfluous for the Greek language but suggest the vowel sounds to the Greek ear? Now at this point we must concede the birth of an idea, an innovation of simple genius which, when grasped, was applied at once and consistently to the conversion of all the requisite signs for the Greek vowels. In an instant the Greek alphabet was born.

What must be stressed is that the act which created the alphabet is an idea, an act of intellect, which so far as signs for the independent consonants are concerned, is also an act of abstraction from anything an ear can hear or a voice say. For the pure consonant (*t*, *d*, *k*, or whatever) is unpronounceable without adding to it some suggestion of vocalic breath. The Phoenician sign stood for a consonant *plus any vowel*, the vowel being supplied from context by a reader. The Greek sign, and this for the first time in the history of writing, stands for an abstraction, the isolated consonant. The phonetic dissolution of the syllable permitted the severance of the consonant from the vowel, and once so freed, signs superfluous to the Greek situation, the signs for the Semitic weak consonants, could be attached to the appropriate vowels.

This act could hardly have been accomplished for one vowel and not for others. This would be equivalent to suggesting that some Greek could grasp the "idea" of the acrophonic principle, the way in which the Semitic word which is meaningless in Greek suggests the pronunciation of a letter of the alphabet, but that the same clever Greek was able to apply the idea only to half of the abecedarium. Surely the intellectual idea of an alphabet, once grasped, would be applied consistently and at once to the Greek vowel sounds *a, e, o*, and even *i*, by any mind clever enough to have invented the device in the first place. I submit that there was no developmental period for the conversion of the signs for the weak consonants to signs for the vowels, and should one day in the future an inscription turn up providing evidence for one, nothing (*pace* Professor Gelb) would surprise me more.

An examination of the first Greek inscriptions, beginning with the Dipylon, probably the oldest of them, reveals that they are the records of private acts, initially rather spontaneous. I conclude that they may be an imitation of what the contemporary Phoenicians, with whom the Greeks were in continual contact, could accomplish by means of a script in their culture. Had Greeks borrowed the Phoenician letters in order to record simple economic ledger prose, no doubt they would have adopted the script "as is" on the Principle of Conservatism: writing systems are adopted *en bloc*, and structural development is later and a response to expanded needs.[18] But if what the Greek wished to do was to record epic speech in a visual medium with precision over the sequence of the vowels equal to the precision and virtuosity of the oral original, then in predictable ways he would have to adapt as well as adopt the mother script.

Instead of Astarte and Ba'al the Greek naturally chose to invoke Apollo or Aphrodite and instead of the rhythmic parallelism of Semitic poetic speech the Greek naturally preferred the formulae of epic or Homeric speech. In order to perform a very old task (preserve orally formulated material) in a new and better way the Greek did indeed borrow a superior technology from his Semitic neighbors, a script. But if I am not mistaken it was the conversion of that technology to the special needs of recording Greek poetry on some enduring substance which provoked into existence the world's first complete alphabet.

NOTES AND REFERENCES

[1] George E. Mylonas, "Prehistoric Greek Scripts," *Archaeology*, Vol. 4, (1948) p. 210.
[2] The definitive work for some time to come is likely to be L.H. Jeffrey, *The Local Scripts of Archaic Greece* (Oxford, 1961). The pioneer work on the late date of the Greek adoption was Rhys Carpenter, "The Antiquity of the Greek Alphabet," *American Journal of Archaeology* (AJA), xxxviii (1933).
[3] The theory that Al Mina was the place of invention has been championed by R.M. Cook and A.G. Woodhouse, *AJA*, lxiii, (1959). Miss Jeffrey, in the Addenda to *Local Scripts*, (p. 374) suggests Al Mina "or in that general area" as the place for adoption. The assumption of a mercantile motive behind the adoption, together with the need for a place of established Greek-Phoenician intercourse, seems to govern the choice of

Al Mina. But no writing of any sort has as yet turned up at Al Mina; moreover pottery remains demonstrate that Al Mina was in earlier and closer economic involvement with Cyprus than with any other part of the Greek world. For the early and extensive character of Phoenician mercantile enterprise, cf. W.F. Albright, "The Role of the Canaanites in the History of Civilization," in G. Wright (ed.), *The Bible and the Ancient Near East* (New York, 1966). In this work and elsewhere Professor Albright argues that Cyprus was the earliest Phoenician mercantile settlement. It certainly was the most important and developed Phoenician community which had direct Greek neighbors and with which all Greek cities had reason to remain in close contact.

[4] I cannot here argue the controversial question of whether the Phoenician script is rightly designated syllabic (as E.A. Havelock, Ignace Gelb, and others have argued), or alphabetic, as many Semiticists designate it. On this point see Havelock's note in *Preface to Plato* (New York, 1967), p. 129, and his references, especially Householder in *Classical Journal* 54, (1959). But I cannot agree with Householder that the Linear B syllabary (which one expert recently described as little better than an "elaborate mnemonic") would have been adequate to record Homeric verse. For such a purpose it would have been inferior to the Phoenician script. See Kevin Robb, "Oral Bards at Mycenae," *Coranto IX*, (1974).

[5] For more extensive analysis and reconstruction, see Kevin Robb, "The Dipylon Prize Graffito," *Coranto*, VII (1971); E.A. Havelock, "The Preliteracy of the Greeks," *New Literary History*, Vol. viii (1976–1977), pp. 370–378.

[6] L.M. Jeffrey's statement (*Local Scripts*, p. 68) is authoritative and concise: "The date of this type of oinochoe should be somewhere in the second half of the eighth century, and it still remains the only example of pottery found in Attica which is certainly Geometric and also carries an undoubted inscription." For this jug in relation to the last stages of Geometric work, see Rodney Young's discussion in *Hesperia*, Suppl. 2 (1939), pp. 228–31. The graffito has no parallels from Attica which can be placed in the Geometric period, and Miss Jeffrey argues that the inscriber must therefore have been a visitor (she suggests from Al Mina) who incised the vase as a gesture of his virtuosity with a newly acquired and locally unfamiliar skill. Much of her reasoning is persuasive, although the concession to the local dialect in the third word remains awkward. Miss Jeffrey's point that this inscription is aberrant in many ways, and that the alphabet could not have been firmly established in Attica as early as ca. 725, is surely correct.

[7] In general see E.A. Havelock, *Prologue to Greek Literacy*, (University of Cincinnati, 1971), and Kevin Robb, *The Progress of Literacy in Ancient Greece*, (Los Angeles, 1971). For the implications of this research for the history of philosophy see Kevin Robb, "Greek Oral Memory and the Origins of Philosophy," *The Personalist* 51 Winter (1971), pp. 5–45, a treatment influenced by evidence advanced earlier primarily by Milman Parry and Eric Havelock.

[8] For a convenient assessment and summary, cf. Denys Page, "Archilochus and the Oral Tradition," *Entrétiens Hardt*, 8 (1963). I exclude as evidence such finds as the Thera stones or Hymettos sherds because no decisive conclusions can be drawn from them. Carl Blegen's assessment of the yield of the Hymettos sherds (twenty-two inscribed pieces from thousands of fragments of pottery) deserves notice: ". . . meager, comprising two names, a vituperative graffito, and two (or perhaps three) childishly incomplete abecedaria." The latter are designated "evidently trial pieces, naive experiments, belonging to a period when the knowledge of writing was beginning to

spread." Carl Blegen, "Inscriptions from Geometric Pottery from Hymettos," *AJA* xxxviii (1934), p. 26. Blegen concludes, strictly on epigraphic grounds, that the Hymettos inscriptions must be somewhat later than the Dipylon graffito. The alphas on the Hymettos inscriptions, for example, are upright, whereas the Dipylon alphas, possibly in imitation of similar Phoenician practice, are on their sides.

9 J.M. Solá-Solé, "Nueva inscripción fenicia de España," (*Hispania* 14), *Rivista degli studi orientali* 41 (Rome 1966), pp. 97–108; Pls. I and II. Frank M. Cross, "The Old Phoenician Inscription from Span Dedicated to Hurrian Astarte," *Harvard Theological Review*, 64 (1971) provides a facsimile from photographs and English translation.

10 Cf. P. Friedlander and H.B. Hoppieit, *Epigrammata* (Berkeley and Los Angeles, 1948), p. 55, p. 38. The statuette is now a part of the collection in the Boston Museum of Fine Arts. The inscription reads: "Mantiklos dedicated me to the Far Darting (god) of the silver bow, out of the tithe. Do you Phoebus (Apollo) give something gracious in return." The inscriber may well have been in the employ of the Theban temple of Apollo (the Ismenion) commissioned to put the new Phoenician letters on such votive offerings for many petitioners. In any case he used a number of chisels and a ring-punch for the circles; the statuette was hardly his only attempt. Mantiklos himself, incidently, may not have been literate, a situation which could well be paralleled for Bal'yaton, his Phoenician near contemporary in Spain. To the Mantiklos inscription also compare the slightly later (ca. 650) inscription of Nicandra to Apollo, written on the right thigh of an archaic female statue. (*IG*, XII, 5, 1425 b). Friedlander notes the "personal and family pride which the example of Homer enables her to express," (*Epigrammata*, p. 49, with the Homeric parallels). Other early comparisons are the inscriptions on the Ischia jug, (G. Buchner and C.F. Russo, *Accademia dei Lincei: Rendiconti* 10, 1955), and the Ithaca cup, (*BSA*, 43, 1948).

11 M.I. Finley's comment on the economics of the situation, especially the Greek need to import metals from Cyprus are, as usual, perceptive. Cf. *Early Greece: The Bronze and Archaic Ages* (New York, 1970), p. 79.

12 The inscription refers to a ritual honoring Astarte, and was found in a temple of which the earliest floor has been dated to 800 B.C. Cf. Andre Dupont-Sommer, "Une inscrition phénicienne archaïque récemment trouvée à Kition" (Chypre), *Mémoires de l'Académie des Inscriptions et Belles Lettres*, tome XLIV (1970), 26 ff. Phoenician inscriptions on Cyprus go back to ca. 900 B.C., the date ascribed to a famous tomb curse tablet first published by A.M. Honeyman, (*Iraq* 6, 1939). The curse invokes the god Ba'al. The earliest Greek parallel is from Camirus on Rhodes, an inscription consisting of one hexameter on either side of a slab of stone, and dated variously to the seventh or sixth century. (*IG*, XII, 1.737). The stone was set over the tomb of one Idameneus, and invokes utter destruction from Zeus on whomever tampers with the tomb. Even the vituperation, however, as Friedlander notes, "echoes epic tone and pride." (*Epigrammata*, p. 36). The next oldest inscription from Cyprus is a dedication to Ba'al Lebanon, and because of reference in it to Hiram, King of the Sidonians, can be dated to 738 B.C. It bears comparison to any of the dozens of early Greek dedicatory inscriptions to various deities. Another early Cypriote curse tablet has been dated by Peckham to ca. 675 B.C. (Brian Peckham, *The Development of the Late Phoenician Scripts*, Cambridge, 1968, p. 16). Next in time follow two short inscriptions on storage jars dated to the beginning and end of the seventh century respectively. They bear comparison in idea (though not in poetic eloquence) to the Dipylon. (Cf. John Myres, *Handbook of the Cesnola Collection of*

Antiquities from Cyprus, New York, 1914, no. 1826 and no. 1827.) These earliest Cypriote inscriptions in the Old Phoenician script are evidence for the sort of uses for writing we can be certain that eighth century Greek traders, craftsmen and minstrels (the classes in society known to be itinerants) must have observed in such established Phoenician colonies as those on Cyprus. They are paralleled (with suitable Greek ad-aptation) in the earliest Greek inscriptions. What may (or may not) have been ob-served by Greeks is the (presumed) Phoenician mercantile uses of writing. Trade, it is conceded, provided the motive for Greek-Phoenician eighth century interaction, and provided as well the routes for the dissemination of letters. From the standpoint of strict logic, however, it does not follow that trade must also have provided the motive for the Greek adoption of Phoenician letters. Also, since an opportunity for observa-tion of a Phoenician practice by Greeks who would also travel the trade routes is the issue, the number of early Greek alphabet inscriptions to turn up on Cyprus is perhaps irrelevant. As for the rivalry between the alphabet and the old Cypriote sylla-bary, the fact that the syllabary possessed signs for the five vowels might be developed into an argument for the Cypriote origin (by stimulus diffusion) of the alphabet. In any case, a silver bowl dated to the seventh century and bearing both a syllabic inscription (in the Paphian signary) and four alphabetic signs (Naucratic) was found in a tomb at Kourion on Cyprus. (New York, Metropolitan Museum, Reg. nos. 74.51.4557, and 4559.)

I thought it best to discuss the complete Cypriote Series in a long footnote rather than to intrude on my text. The evidence is important because (a) Cyprus yields by far the greatest number of inscriptions for the relevant dates, (b) had long established bi-lingual centers, (c) therefore, even if not the *locus* of transfer of the Phoenician letters, provides the best evidence for normal Phoenician practice (whether on Cyprus, on Rhodes, in Spain, or at Karatepe) ca. 750–600 B.C. Cyprus, because of the abun-dance of evidence for precisely the years which concern us, must provide the control for our speculation on what Greek may have observed of Phoenician practice in any part of the Eastern Mediterranean.

[13] Maurice Bowra, *Landmarks of Greek Literature* (London, 1966), pp. 58–59.

[14] In *A Study of Writing* (Chicago, 1952), p. 182.

[15] Delbert Hillers, *Covenant: The History of a Biblical Idea* (Baltimore, 1969), p. 54.

[16] Of course Professor Hillers can not be held responsible for my interpretation of these curses. The formulaic character of the early Phoenician inscriptions is not, incidently, restricted to funeral curses, but has been detected also in the important Karatepe inscription. (CF. Peckham, *Development*, p. 16) and elsewhere. Also cf. St. Givirtz, "West Semitic Curses and the Problem of the Origins of Hebrew Law," *Vetus Tes-tamentum* 11 (1961), pp. 137 ff. Cross noted formulaic elements in the new inscrip-tion to Hurrian Astarte (notably in line four) in the *Harvard Theological Review*, 64 (1971), p. 191. In a personal letter to Friedlander, W.F. Albright observed: "You are quite right in supposing that Phoenician epigraphic formulae closely resembled Greek formulae of the same class." (quoted in *Epigrammata*, p. 7, no. 1.)

[17] The translation is borrowed from Cyprus Gordon who cannot be held responsible for my interpretation. Frank Moore Cross at Harvard, and, in a series of doctoral disserta-tions, his students, have analyzed and documented the structure and oral background of both Ugaritic and Hebrew. Cross begins an important article with the statement: "The myths and epics of Ugarit are composed in poetic formulae and patterns which reveal original oral composition. Parallelistic structure derives, originally at least, from

the techniques of orally composed poetry. . . ." A colophon (CTA 6.6 53 ff) even names both master-singer and scribe at Ugarit, a situation without analogue in Homeric studies. Cf. F.M. Cross, "Prose and Poetry in the mythic and Epic Texts from Ugarit," *Harvard Theological Review*, 67 (1974) pp. 1–15. Add the research of Michael Dahood S.J. of Beirut on the Phoenician background (or at least shared common oral sources) of material which found its way into Hebrew scriptures. Cf. M. Dahood, "The Phoenician Contribution to Biblical Wisdom Literature," in *Papers Presented to the Archaeological Symposium at the American University of Beirut; March, 1977*, (Beirut 1968).

The translators of the King James version of the Bible (1611) were unaware of parallelistic construction as a poetic unit, and hence much poetry was printed as prose. Subsequent editions and translations have attempted corrections but as late as 1927 Goodspeed could defend the need for a new translation, the "Chicago" Bible, partially on the grounds that much that was still being printed as prose in current versions of the Old Testament was in fact in the original Hebrew rhythmical, hence poetic. The translation, he argued, should reveal this and print poetry as such. W.F. Albright, F.M. Cross, and their students have penetrated behind Semitic poetic units which were captured at a point in time in a text to a much older period of oral composition and transmission which may go back time out of mind. They have thereby explained the close affinities between Hebrew and many non-Hebrew (e.g., Canaanite) texts. These derive from a common Semitic "floating" body of such oral poetry. The various versions are thus of extraordinary similarity despite formulation in different Semitic languages in different centuries.

[18] I do not deny that writing often (but not always) is called into existence in response to expanding economic needs. For instance, the great excavator of Uruk, Falkenstein (*Archaische Texte aus Uruk*, Berlin, 1936) has demonstrated how the Sumerian writing system developed from the pictographic to the syllabic stage (where it halted) in response to expanding economic needs such as huge public granaries and a complicated canal system for irrigation. There is similar development in the Cretan writing terminating in the Linear B syllabary. But in such cases (a) the development can be traced in the surviving texts and (b) is in each case just sufficient to meet the economic need, so difficult was the maintenance of any degree of literacy in antiquity. I would argue that the Phoenician unvocalized script was adequate for any economic needs in Greece in the ninth and indeed through the eighth and seventh centuries. No one can of course disprove the theory that some Greek or Greeks (perhaps quite independently of one another) at various times in those centuries may have used the Phoenician letters for some kind of mercantile purposes. There is no evidence for it, but neither is it impossible. But such jottings, if they occurred, can not be made a part of the developmental history of Greek literacy.

JOSEPH RUSSO is Professor of Classics at Haverford College, Haverford, Pennsylvania. He was formerly on the faculty of Yale University and in 1977–78 was Visiting Professor at the University of Michigan. His main interests and publications have centered on Homeric epic and archaic Greek poetry, Greek mythology and comparative mythology, and folklore. He is a member of both the American Philological Association and the American Folklore Society. Currently he is completing a new edition with detailed commentary of Books 17 to 20 of the *Odyssey*, for an edition of the entire *Odyssey* shared by six scholars from five different countries.

How, and What, Does Homer Communicate? The Medium and Message of Homeric Verse[*]

by JOSEPH RUSSO

FORMULAR STYLE AND ORAL STYLE: PROBLEMS OF DEFINITION

MILMAN PARRY'S monumental contribution to Homeric studies taught us to read the *Iliad* and *Odyssey* in a new light.[1] It has also raised some difficult questions. Parry's insights have been extended and elaborated at greatest

[*] An earlier version of this article appeared in *The Classical Journal* (Vol. 71, 1976), to which grateful acknowledgement is made.

length by his former collaborator, Professor Albert Lord, and a host of contributions on specific points have been added by a number of classical scholars.[2] We have been made aware of the traditional nature of Homer's poetry, of the wide-ranging formulaic patterns and systems that contribute to the organization of his verse, and of the role such poetry plays as the vehicle for the transmission and preservation of cultural values in a society that glorifies the great achievements of its heroic past. Still unsettled, however, are such fundamental questions as the adequate definition of the Homeric "formula," and the appropriateness of the analogies to twentieth-century Yugoslav oral heroic narrative and to other traditions of non-literate verse narrative in which comparatists have seen Homeric parallels.

The central issue is this: Parry's studies of Homeric diction and of Yugoslav oral poetry came to the conclusion 1) that "orality" was a distinguishing feature of a large segment of the world's narrative poetry; therefore oral narrative verse was in a special category and must not be criticized or analyzed by the same methods we use on literary poetry; and 2) that this orality depended on a diction that was fundamentally formulary or formulaic, which made possible a mode of recitation that was *to some* degree—although to just what degree is a very moot point—composition and performance rolled into one. Whether Parry really believed the Homeric poems were literally extemporized *de novo* each time they were performed, with no conscious premeditation and rehearsal, is hard to determine. This view *is* affirmed, however, in Professor Lord's writings, based on the analogy of Yugoslav oral poets, and has thus become part of what is called the Parry-Lord theory. Whether what is true for the South Slavic epic was true also for Homer is difficult to answer, and will probably always remain an unresolved question, for lack of more direct testimony concerning Homer. My own view is that common sense is enough to tell us that the *Iliad* and *Odyssey* are *planned* rather than *improvised* poems—if we have only those two positions to choose between. I would suggest that one difficulty with Professor Lord's position on the genesis of Homer's poems is that he gives the impression that these two polar positions are the only two hypotheses available. The likeliest hypothesis seems to be one that allows for improvisitory embellishment or expansion of certain details in the story, but conceives of the two monumental epics as "final versions" that the poet has arrived at through careful planning of the plot structure and lots of rehearsal and practice, certainly in the form of earlier "trial" performances and possibly in the form of conscious practice of various segments.[3]

The central ambiguity, for me, in the Parry-Lord approach is its wish to equate poetic composition that *employs* formulas with the kind of improvised performance that *is completely dependent* on them. There remains an as yet unresolved problem in estimating the relationship between formularity and orality in traditional poetry of this sort, and in making such a judgement specifically about Homer. The orthodox Parry-Lord position is that a poet must be truly formular in order to be truly oral and vice versa.[4] Such a tight connection between orality and formularity seems right and proper if our model is to be Serbo-Croatian heroic poetry, which does happen to be highly formular and has been observed to be oral-improvisatory in its style of composition. Objections have been raised, however, by scholars familiar with other traditions of oral composition, such as the Celtic. In Irish and Scots Gaelic oral verse there is less dependence on the repetition of formulas and formula-patterns, and far more careful, premeditated composition inside the poet's head before he recites.[5] If you can be oral, then, without being formulaic, it may well be that you can be formulaic without being oral; and the large body of hexametric Greek poetry from the archaic period suggests that this became the case at some point. The Homeric Hymns, Theognis, the early elegists, and pieces of epic from lost poems of the epic cycle and later poets like Panyassis, all use many formulas and formulaic expressions or formula-patterns in their hexameters, and yet it is very likely that most of this poetry is not truly oral. What obviously happened was that at some point poets begin composing with careful premeditation, and perhaps the help of writing, but what they had to say was still best said in what remained essentially the old formular style. It is impossible to pinpoint *where* this happened in the Greek poetic tradition; and it is at least possible that it happened *as early as Homer himself.*

Professor Lord points out that when this happens in the Yugoslav tradition he can always distinguish such literate imitations from the true oral formular verse by the sheer *quantity* or *percentage* of formulas used; and he has transferred this quantitative approach to the analysis of Homeric poetry. But I am not sure that the transfer can be made. It seems to me that the test for formular percentage in Homer cannot have any claim to authority unless we know two things for certain (neither of which we really know): 1) what percentage of formula-dependency in *this* tradition, i.e. the Greek, makes the poet *so* formula-dependent that we can be sure he needed them for fluency in an improvising situation;[6] and 2) what, exactly, is a formula?

FROM ORAL TO AURAL

There have been a variety of definitions offered for the formula, and it is not worth our time reviewing them here.[7] I would rather take a new tack on the issue of the formula and say that there has been a basic misconception in our quest for the correct definition, in that we tended to view the different definitions or kinds of formulas as *competing* with one another, and we thought that our task was to find the single correct one. The answer may be, simply, that all the definitions are right: they all correctly identify a particular reality, i.e., a certain level of regularity in the language the poet uses to convey his meaning to his audience. There are formulas operating simultaneously on different levels of language when the poet is reciting his poem to the audience, and our task must be to understand how each serves the purpose of *com-*

munication between poet and listener. Each kind of formula communicates something special *and appropriate to the level on which it operates,* and the levels range from the purely sonorous and rhythmic up through the semantic, the thematic, and beyond. All these formulas are *aural:* they are a set of overlapping structures that serve communication and take their meaning from the act of being spoken and heard. Whether they are also *oral* in the narrower sense found in Yugoslav poetry—i.e. as the necessary composing devices for oral ex tempore composition—is a question that I think we can no longer meaningfully address.[8]

The Limits of Form

Where does the argument I have presented thus far lead? I see it leading us in two directions, describable simply as inwards and outwards: inwards, into the nature of the hexameter line itself, and outwards into some general truths about the epic genre and how it differs from prose narrative.

The Greek epic poet worked in a different medium from those who composed in other genres. This medium was the dactylic hexameter verse, which imposed limitations which we can view as the foundation for—and eventually in a more complex relation to—every other distinguishing feature of epic poetry. Unlike the lyric poets or the early epodes composed by Archilochus, the Greek epic poet could not alter or play around with the formal structure of the verse he inherited from his tradition. And upon this tight adherence to *form,* other strong traditional associations are built. If we consider, for example, the English poets who composed epics or long verse narratives similar to epics, we see that although the tradition called for a five-beat (iambic) line, they are in fact much freer than Homer, much less bound to copy the exact verse-forms of their predecessors. We do not need to span many years to collect examples of this freedom: look at the iambic pentameter of Pope, Dryden and Milton, and see how much leeway there was in their composition; not just in technical "internal" matters like placement of caesura, use of elision, prose stress versus verse ictus, and so on, but in large or gross features like rhyming or not, composing in couplets or not. And there was, moreover, the possibility, at least at a slightly earlier period, of following the different, well-established European tradition and composing, like Spenser, by stanzas rather than by the single line, which brought in not only the metrically longer final line but also the need to move the narrative along by these large stanzaic units and round the thought off periodically in the longer closing line.

The Greek poet, however, once he dons the mantle of epic speech under the patronage of his *Mousa,* is committed to dactylic hexameter and all that it demands. And it demands a lot, as we shall see. The poet is committing himself to speak like his predecessors, like his ancestors. Seen in this dimension the commitment is a culturally sacred one; no wonder then that the bonds are especially strict. The poet is committing himself linguistically, psychologically, socially, and finally, in a sense, ideologically; that is, he is committing himself to a world-view that is as complete as it is limited. The commitment, or set of bonds, can be seen as a structure of *regularities*, regularities operating simultaneously on various levels. It will be easy to see that they complement and reinforce one another. I should like, after describing them, to try to pose the question of their relationship in still stronger terms. There is a sense in which they not only need each other, but, if I may so put it, they *mean* each other. We shall return to this shortly. First, the regularities themselves, or what I have termed the "Five Levels of Regularity." We shall read them from lowest to highest.

FIVE LEVELS OF REGULARITY

At the ground level, so to speak, of the hexameter is what was once neatly labelled the *outer metric*.[9] This is simply the most external formal requirement: the use of dactylic rhythm terminating in either a natural or enforced spondee. The poet must use five dactyls any one of which may have a spondaic substitution, with an inhibition (but not prohibition) on having a spondee replace the fifth dactyl. Growing out of—or working its way into, if you prefer that metaphor—this outer metric is what O'Neill called the *inner metric* or *rhythmical metric*: the complicated set of rhythmical inhibitions known to graduate students in classics as that set of "laws" bearing the names of German scholars of the nineteenth and early twentieth centuries. Their authority reaches out over the centuries, forbidding the ancient poets' use of a trochaic word that ends in the fourth foot or a heavy-footed spondaic word confined entirely within that foot, or a word-end at the exact midpoint of the verse, the end of the third foot, unless there is also a word end put in its proper caesural position one or two syllables earlier *within* that third foot; and so on. While they may seem arbitrary to the beginning student or amateur, to the professional student of Greek poetry these rhythmical inhibitions are actually very intriguing. They appear in fairly rigid form in the earliest hexameter poetry, Homer's, and stay and grow increasingly rigid in later hexameter, so that Callimachus and Theocritus appear as the height of rhythmical refinement compared to Homer.

Where these "laws" for avoided and favored word-ending came from in the first place is hard to say. Metricians tend to present them as rules of the hexameter structure itself; but I suspect they arose first as a result of repeated formula groupings that became habitual, and then by their frequent presence took on the authority of norms, and then finally (codified by German scholarship) "laws."[10] It is important to stress their positive function, as norms for preferred word-ending at definite points within the verse, rather than viewing them all negatively as prohibitions on the use of certain word-types at certain places. This allows us to see an important feature of articulation within the structure of the hexameter: the tendency for preferred word-end, or caesura, at three main points to create a line based on four short segments, or *cola*. This articulation of the verse into *cola* has been carefully documented, and in fact represents a small but well-developed recent tradition within Homeric and metrical scholarship. What is singularly important for our examination is the fact that these four cola often serve as the formal limits within which Homer's familiar formular phraseology is contained.[11]

My third regularity, working upward, is *diction*. The poet's choice of words is limited to a great extent to a stock of time-honored, well-established words, set phrases, and familiar phrasal patterns. Growing out of these is a range of expressions—single words or phrases *structured* similarly or even phrases that *sound* alike but have different syntax and sense—that the poet chooses *by analogy* to the words and phrases already in the stock diction. The fluency and possibility for variation and new expression offered by the play of analogy is of great value to the poet when he wants to go beyond outright repetition of what is already in the tradition; and Professor Lord's chapter on the Formula in *The Singer of Tales* is an important statement of the possibilities offered by formulaic analogy in an oral tradition. Now that we are on the level of phrase patterning or structure, it is important to note that the colometric four-part structure of the verse mentioned above serves as the mould into which any newly formed phrase patterns must be fit; although it was the strong presence of favored phrase patterns, as suggested earlier, that may have been decisive in creating the colometric structure to begin with. This pre-historical interplay of meter and formula must remain a mystery. The important point is that once either of these formal structures gained a foothold it would have tended to attract the other and strengthen it; so the issue is not to decide the priority of either but to appreciate their mutually reinforcing roles.

Fourth of my regularities is *theme* or *incident*. We now have moved up from *metric*, *rhythm* (a simple way to distinguish and label the first two levels), and *diction* (which includes phrase-patterns), to the level where language is organized into a *story* by the poet and enjoyed as sequential narrative by the listeners. As on the level of diction the poet dealt with an available stock of set and ready-made patterns within which there could be variation, so too on the level of story or plot the poet has as his conscious purpose the retelling of established tales, the manipulation and combination of known patterns. Thematic composition is, then, like formular composition in the way it allows for *invention* within the framework of *tradition*, thus harmonizing these two apparently contradictory impulses. If we try to make exact estimates of how much tradition and how much invention the poet uses, either in general or in any specific passage, different Homeric scholars tend to come up with different estimates. What we all agree on is that there are many formulas and much use of thematic composition. Arguing just how much, and therefore how binding it is on the poet's storytelling habits and on the verbal habits that serve as their underpinning, is the issue that has found no agreement among specialists and may well deserve to be called the new American Homeric Question. But the great insight brought by Parry's work is that we have become aware that the poet's storytelling habits depend very much upon his verbal habits, and we must ponder the question whether storytelling itself is just one verbal habit writ large. If so, and we would probably all grant it is so to a serious degree, we are entitled to see a perfect continuum up from the verbal or formular level—and beneath that the colometric and rhythmic level and the metric level on which the whole structure rests—up to the level of story or plot at which the normal member of the audience perceives the poetic performance. What he perceives, by my argument, is just the tip of the iceberg; and my special point is that the iceberg is of a very consistent texture and structure all the way up, from base to tip. I can best show what that means by going to my fifth level of regularity, which I call *outlook*.

THE EPIC OUTLOOK

The traditional epic poet, reciting before his audience, must hold out to them a coherent world-picture, with everything in its place. (The first draft of this paper, used for oral presentation, contained the verbal error "word-picture" for "world picture," a very revealing slip because it offers the most effective symbolization of the point at issue!)[12] Such a world picture shows certain unvarying constants. Men should be in their proper ranks and roles in society, with the proper behavior and values carried out at each rank; the Olympian gods should be performing their customary roles, whether on Olympus or in the world of men, as guardians of those special virtues and chosen individuals that they customarily support; and against this background of all things in their proper positions and attitudes we should have the unfolding of a plot that moves to its proper outcome. By "proper" I do not mean that good triumphs in the end or that all problems are successfully solved (this literature is too mature for such easy formulas). I mean an outcome that validates and reinforces a variety of beliefs held by the poet's audience.[13] Central among these are the religious and quasi-philosophical values and social values held, and the personal values imagined or pretended to, by the listener.

I like to see my five levels as forming a unity, a coherent whole. Hence the appropriateness of my slip, word-picture for world-picture, because for the epic poet the word *is* the world, the world he describes by his poetry. Now I know in a sense this is true for everyone: we are all symbolizing creatures, and speech is our great symbolizing device. My point is that this is more perfectly true, admitting of fewer qualifications or exceptions, for the epic poet. The truism that risks dissolving into a pure metaphor for us becomes reality for him. His epic world takes its reality from the special kind of language in which he describes it. It is describable only as a word-product, a linguistic construct, and the special nature of that language is necessary to create the special nature of the epic world. While we all need words to describe our realities, we can go some way towards apprehending them in non-verbal ways as well, since their existence is not absolutely contingent upon our verbal evocation of them; but there is no other way to bring the heroic world of epic into being except through a combination of those elements of familiar regularity on the levels of metre, rhythm, diction, incident, and outlook in the performance of an epic bard. That world exists only so long as the bard chants. In that world men are earthbound, *epichthonioi anthrōpoi*, grain eaters, *siton edontes*, and when presented in this their fundamental nature they always close the verse and the thought sequence. Their most stable, quintessential characteristics, as represented by the traditional epithets, happen to find expression in the most metrically stable part of the verse, the closing two to two-and-a-half feet. This conjunction is no accident, or is the kind of happy accident that makes it a meaningful one. The gods' epithets have more variety than those of mortals, but they also regularly come at the close of a rhythmic and thought sequence, that is, at the end of a verse. These epithets describe what is permanent or inescapable about the gods or men, or other nouns representing a constant presence in the epic world, such as spears or shields or ships or the sea or bronze or the sky or mountains or wine etc etc. These objects or people may do a variety of other things in the narrative, but one central truth about Poseidon, for example, is that he causes earthquakes, hence he is *ennosigaios*; and bronze in weapons is always, ultimately, pitiless when it is driven against human skin, hence *nēlei chalkōi*: and not in the middle of the verse do these things have these qualities, but at the end, as the closing act of the miniature dramatic movement that is the long hexameter line. Epic verse in its very structure moves from the variables and unpredictables to the inescapable and fixed facts about man and the universe of gods and objects that he lives in, as the epic verse winds its way rhythmically from the first to the fourth colon.

I note in passing that this view of the epic line, which emphasizes the rigidity and predictability of rhythm (recall the tendency to avoid spondees in the fifth foot) and of language at the *end* of the verse, contrasted with a relative semantic and rhythmic openness in the early part of the line, has been endorsed by scholars working in comparative linguistics and seeking the Indo-European origins of the hexameter verse. An interesting recent paper by K. O'Nolan, in *Classical Quarterly* for 1969, compares Homer with Irish heroic (prose) narrative and argues that in both Greek and Irish epic traditions the descriptive epithets are the oldest part of the diction. O'Nolan goes on to suggest, following Calvert Watkins' work with Indo-European metrics and archaic Irish verse,[14] that it was the tail end of the Greek epic line that first took on a final fixed rhythmical form, and the rest of the line then followed. Such a phenomenon is both linguistically likely (since end-line epithets preserve many linguistic archaisms) and has been turned to maximum aesthetic advantage by the epic poet's verbal art.

Regularity vs. Possibility: The Epic and the Novel

What I have offered might be called an *esthetic of regularity* in every aspect of epic storytelling in verse, an esthetic built on the satisfactions of recurrence. If we think of the rhythmic movement of the line, the repeated use of familiar formula-based language, and the re-telling of stories already told before, we can see that a prime emotional bond holding the attention and admiration of the epic audience is the re-assurance gained from the guarantee of *recurrence*, a recurrence that occurs on several levels of formal organization of language. The word recurrence is Northrop Frye's key term for identifying the movement of epic language. Epos is characterized by what he calls "the rhythm of recurrence" and prose fiction, in contrast, by the "rhythm of continuity." [15] These are fine and accurate terms; but to bring out the contrast between the idiosyncratic qualities of the two genres involved—especially if we are emphasizing the content of the story as well as the energy of the language that tells it, as I have been—I would modify the terms and say instead that epic offers the cyclic rhythm of regularity or predictability and prose fiction offers the more linear rhythm of open-ended possibility. Consider the wide variety in the way novels are composed nowadays. The story-teller in prose fiction can do just about anything; any world can be created for which the author can find the language, and since many creative ways are found to use language, so are there many kinds of original and experimental novels in evidence. The story can go anywhere, just as the sentence can go anywhere and be as long as it wants with whatever rhythm it wants—no adonic clausula, no spondee to watch out for lest it get in your fifth foot, no Hermann's law, and no elaborate repertoire of formulas to help sustain fluent composition. A tradition-bound Greek would find the novel intolerable: too much possibility. Our own contemporaries, on the other hand, read few epics and compose none. The esthetic of limited possibilities is not attractive to the modern spirit.

From the "Eccentric" to the Center

The action of the *Iliad* and *Odyssey* tends to move away from the proliferation of possibilities and toward a progressive narrowing of choice, toward the inevitable. This narrowing may be seen on the large-scale level of plot as well as on the smaller levels of theme, diction, rhythm, and metre, as the embodiment of that preference, discussed above, for a design that moves from the variable to the secure, from the lesser to the greater certainty. The story, like the verse structure, progresses toward what we may call the triumph of the normative over the deviant, of the long-range "proper" resolution over the temporary atypical situation. We see this pattern not only in the large design that overarches the entire epic poem—the reconciliation of Achilles with Agamemnon's leadership and with his own unavoidable destiny, the return of Odysseus to his homeland and his final vengeance on the Suitors—but also in many of the subsidiary incidents that fill out the story. A perfect example of the pattern is seen in the *Iliad's* second book, in the unexpected outbreak of disorder caused by the speech in which Agamemnon proposes that the Greeks give up the war and leave Troy, his intention being to trick the Greeks by testing their morale. In a spontaneous and anarchic over-reaction to the speech, the entire army rushes to the ships and begins to embark. The goddess Athena, however, sent by Hera, comes to Odysseus and urges him to run among the men and persuade them to return. He manages this successfully, the tide is turned, and the army is finally brought back to re-form their assembly. Such an episode represents the momentary outbreak of the eccentric, of the deviant action, which is finally subdued as the eccentricity is brought back into line with what is proper and normative in the social, military, and political order. The divine order is also served, since Hera emphatically maintains her long-range goal, punishment of the Trojans, through the agency of the Achaeans, for the original offence given her by the famous Judgement of Paris, in which the Trojan prince rejected Hera's offer of political power in favor of the love of Helen offered by Aphrodite. [16] The shape of this interesting incident is controlled by the concern to maintain the social and political fabric of the Greek host and the historic and moral design that guarantees Troy's ultimate defeat. Homer has skilfully created this eccentric incident to embarrass Agamemnon, to undermine our respect for the king's judgement and authority by showing that Zeus himself has enjoyed tricking the Achaean leader. And yet the Greeks must continue to function as an organized society, and their ultimate purpose, the capture of Troy, must be sustained. Inevitably, then, the incident concludes with a return to the correct order of things.

If this incident can be taken as paradigmatic of a larger pattern, that larger pattern is seen in the story that runs from the first to the twenty-fourth book of the *Iliad*. Summarily stated, it is the story of a schism in the Greek leadership, Achilles' military and political defection—this public or external act of withdrawal having an internal concomitant in Achilles' psychological withdrawal from the value-system of epic heroism—and his eventual return to the system, when the consequences of defection have brought personal tragedy and forced him to accept the political leadership (and apology) of Agamemnon as well as the personal destiny (a short but glorious life) that he had sought to deny. In this narrative design we see the same essential pattern we saw in the smaller incident: the ultimate triumph of the normative over the deviant, the surrender of the atypical to the most traditional, most secure, most reassuring rhythms of society, of life, of destiny itself. A major function of the *Iliad*, from the sociological-contextual rather than the literary-esthetic point of view, is to reinforce the belief system of those who hear the poem recited: belief in what I have called the fifth and highest level of regularity, that of a reliable and consistent social and cosmic scheme.

The plot of the *Odyssey* serves the same purpose, through a similar structural scheme: the progress of Odysseus, through a sequence of adventures, away from the eccentric and marginal position of a king, husband, and father who has been separated from the social and political structures and the personal relationships that define these roles, and back to the Ithacan center at which he belongs and from which he began.

My argument, then, is that a certain "message" is repeatedly communicated by these epic poems to their intended audiences by means of the structures employed at different levels of organization of language. At the levels of metre, rhythm, and diction, this message is best equated with an "esthetic of regularity." At the level of story and world-view, the same message might be better described as the constant yielding of the eccentric to the superior gravitational pull of the center. The epic plot generates its tension, and hence its interest *qua* narrative, in the momentary creation of the atypical or marginal situation and the struggle to re-incorporate this back into the social, political, and cosmic normalities. From this perspective, the movement of epic may seem to parallel that of rituals of passage, whose three stages were described in Arnold van Gennep's classic study as "separation," "margin," and "incorporation."[17] Since epic story-telling is essentially a social, public performance and not a "literary" product like our modern narrative fiction, it should not surprise us to find that its underlying structural pattern is akin to that of ritual.

CONCLUSION

I have tried to show how both the language and the form of early Greek epic were shaped to function with special effect as a medium of communication. Epic became the medium *par excellence* for communicating a set of multiple, reciprocally reinforcing messages—both explicit and implicit in the narrative, and constantly implicit in the rhythms and formulaic patterns of the epic diction—to a society that saw in the epic a mirror of itself and of the world around it. It was no ordinary mirror, but one designed to give back idealized, powerfully attractive, and easily retained images. These images functioned as messages, emanating as it were from the society's past and from its normative center, and serving to maintain commonly shared assumptions and values by emphasizing the historical precedents and ideal paradigms on which these values were based, thereby guaranteeing their validity and vigor for an age not yet affected by the disruptive questionings of philosophers like Xenophanes and Heraclitus, of the Sophists, and finally Socrates. Perhaps we can find a better metaphor than that of the mirror if we decide to call the epic an encyclopedia;[18] or perhaps the best metaphor is language itself, in so far as language is the conceptual medium that conveys our information while at the same time it shapes and limits the ways in which we perceive and understand it.

If epic, then, is a special kind of language, what our analysis has shown is that this language has been specially designed, through a combination of historical, social, and sociolinguistic demands made upon it, to communicate through a multi-levelled structure of controlling forms based on the patterns of recurrence and regularity. The much-discussed Homeric formula is, among these forms, the one that is most immediately conspicuous and has received most attention in recent (especially American) scholarship. But the formula, as we have seen, is only one member of a cohesive hierarchy of forms. The special power of this hierarchic structure called epic poetry derives from the perfect success with which its constituent levels have been integrated, by the poetic genius of generations of anonymous artists in the medium of verbal symbolic form, to communicate a vision of reality that held good for centuries.

NOTES AND REFERENCES

[1] Parry's writings are now available in a single volume, edited with an excellent introductory essay by his son Adam Parry: *The Making of Homeric Verse: the Collected Papers of Milman Parry*, ed. Adam Parry (Oxford Univ. Press, 1971).

[2] Lord's major contribution is *The Singer of Tales* (Cambridge [Mass.]: Harvard Univ. Press, 1960). Other scholarship in the Parry tradition is well summarized in Adam Parry's Introduction to *The Making of Homeric Verse*. For the problems raised by Parry's methodology, see A. Hoekstra, *Homeric Modifications of Formulaic Prototypes* (Amsterdam: North-Holland Publishing Company, 1965), Chapter 1. For the problems bequeathed to literary criticism, see F. M. Combellack, "Milman Parry and Homeric Artistry," *Comparative Literature* 11 (1959) 193–208; Joseph Russo, "Homer Against his Tradition," *Arion* 7 (1968) 275–295; J.B. Hainsworth, "The Criticism of an Oral Homer," *Journal of Hellenic Studies* 90 (1970) 90–98.

[3] Hainsworth's discussion (above, n. 2) concludes with a similar distinction between the more typically "oral" parts of Homer's epics and the carefully planned larger dramatic structure.

[4] "Truly formular" remains, unfortunately, a floating concept that still resists precise definition (see n. 6 below). J.A. Notopoulos has found 23% of the Hesiodic corpus to consist of repetitions and 33% of the Homeric, and he finds these proportions a clear indicator of oral style: "Homer, Hesiod, and the Achaean Heritage of Oral Poetry," *Hesperia* 29 (1960) 180. A.B. Lord, on the other hand, in his recent study "Homer as Oral Poet," *Harvard Studies in Classical Philology* 72 (1967) 24, says "50 to 60 percent formula or formulaic, with 10 to perhaps 25 per cent straight formula, indicates clearly literary or written composition." Since "straight formula" must mean verbatim formula or repetition, Hesiod would be oral by Notopoulos' criterion and written by

Lord's. Homer, with 33% formular repetition, would be truly oral if we accept either of these quantitative measurements.

[5] This objection is raised most vehemently by Douglas Young, "Never Blotted a Line? Formula and Premeditation in Homer and Hesiod," *Arion* 6 (1967) 279–324. See also K. O'Nolan, "Homer and Irish Heroic Epic Poetry," *Classical Quarterly* 19 (1969) 18 n. 3; G.L. Huxley, *Greek Epic Poetry from Eumelos to Panyassis* (Cambridge [Mass.]: Harvard Univ. Press, 1969) 191–196 ("Appendix: Some Irish Analogies").

[6] This question was raised pointedly by J.B. Hainsworth in "Structure and Content in Epic Formulae: the Question of the Unique Expression," *Classical Quarterly* 14 (1964) 155–164, esp. p. 158. In my article "The Structural Formula in Homeric Verse," *Yale Classical Studies* 20 (1966) 219–240, which is in part a reply to Hainsworth, I took the position that a "very high" degree of formulaic usage and patterning was a sufficient indication of oral style. But since my conception of oral style was looser than Lord's, and was essentially that of an "orally-evolved style" (234) rather than of an oral-improvisatory compositional technique, my position and Hainsworth's are not in direct conflict.

[7] A good review is given by Michael Nagler, "Towards a Generative View of the Homeric Formula," *Transactions of the American Philological Association* 98 (1967) 269–280. Nagler goes on to give a definition that moves the formula out of the realm of verbal phenomena, or "surface structure," and into the deeper (and more obscure) area designated by the concepts "mental template" and "pre-verbal Gestalt." A more developed presentation of this argument is made in the first two chapters of Nagler's *Spontaneity and Tradition* (Berkeley: Univ. of California Press, 1974).

[8] The aura/oral relationship is discussed at length in my article "Is Aural or Oral Composition the Cause of Homer's Formulaic Style?" in Stolz and Shannon (eds.), *Oral Literature and the Formula*, Ann Arbor, 1976.

[9] See Eugene O'Neill, Jr., "The Localization of Metrical Word-Types in the Greek Hexameter," *Yale Classical Studies* 8 (1942) 105, n. 2, for definitions of inner and outer metric.

[10] This view was expressed in "The Structural Formula in Homeric Verse" (above, note 6), and is shared by Gregory Nagy, *Comparative Studies in Greek and Indic Meter* (Cambridge [Mass.]: Harvard University Press, 1974) 8f., See also O'Nolan (above, note 5) 14.

[11] See the "Appendix of Common Structural Formulas" (pp. 236–240) to my article cited above, note 6. This idea is borrowed and amplified by W.B. Ingalls, "Another Dimension of the Homeric Formula," *Phoenix* 26 (1972) 111–122.

[12] It is interesting to note that this same slip, equating "word" with "world," was exploited by an epic craftsman of a later age for whom the word also had the power to create a world. In James Joyce's *Ulysses*, the slip is made in the letter from Martha Clifford, the typist, to Leopold Bloom ("I do not like that other world"). This slip is so natural and obvious that proofreaders of the earliest editions of *Ulysses* constantly "corrected" it, changing "world" back to "word" and thus undoing the Freudian slip that Joyce had so cleverly contrived.

[13] What I call the validating and reinforcing of epic story-telling in a traditional society is a phenomenon much described by anthropologists when discussing traditional tales and myths. Among the classic statements on the subject, see, for example, B. Malinowski, *Myth in Primitive Psychology* (London 1926), who shows how tale-telling can function as social charter and legitimizer, and as a protective screen against the threat-

ening aspect of the unknown; and Clyde Kluckhohn, "Myth and Ritual: A General Theory" (*Harvard Theological Review* 35 [1942] 45–79), who stresses how myth serves the psychological function of alleviating anxiety and offers, together with ritual, an unremitting source of the gratification that comes from the expected and habitual.

14 "Indo-European Metrics and Archaic Irish Verse," *Celtica* 6 (1963) 194–249. Commenting on the "longer Irish line" whose syllabic length corresponds to the Indo-European longer line as reflected in Vedic, Greek, and Slavic, Watkins notes: "We have the same organization into three cola, with progressive fixation leading to an invariant third colon (with final anceps), the cadence." (244).

15 *Anatomy of Criticism* (Princeton, New Jersey: Princeton University Press, 1957; Princeton Paperback Edition, 1971) 251ff.

16 Note Hera's statement at *Iliad* II.155–65, and cf. IV.25–36 and XXIV.25–30.

17 A. van Gennep, *The Rites of Passage*, tr. M. Vizedom and G. Caffee (University of Chicago Press, 1960), pp. 10–11 for this fundamental distinction, *passim* for illustrations. For the equation of certain Odyssean themes with van Gennep's categories, see Charles Segal, "Transition and Ritual in Odysseus' Return," in *La Parola del Passato* 40 (1967) 321–342.

18 I owe this metaphor to Eric Havelock, *Preface to Plato* (Cambridge, Mass.: Harvard University Press, 1963), ch. IV, "The Homeric Encyclopedia."

GEORGE N. GORDON is the only contributor to this collection who is not a classicist, although, at the not-so-gentle urging of his father, a New York magistrate, his six-year studies of Latin took him as far as the letters of Horace. This pursuit was, however, interrupted by military service during World War II, after which Dr. Gordon attended the Yale Drama School and, during a short career as a professional actor, appeared in English translations of *Antigone*, *Oedipus at Colonus* and various versions of Plautus' *Amphitryo* including the latest, Jean Giraudoux's *Amphitryon 38*. He is the author or co-author of fifteen books on contemporary mass communications including *Persuasion, The Theory and Practice of Manipulative Communications* (Hastings House, 1971) and *The Communications Revolution* (Hastings House, 1977). At present he serves as chairperson of the Communication Arts Department at Hofstra University in Hempstead, New York and is General Editor of Hastings House's *Humanistic Studies in the Communication Arts*. He is now working on a critical and analytic study of erotic communications, that, he claims, will pay proper attention to the contributions of Greece and Rome to these arcana.

Aristotle as a
Modern Propagandist

by GEORGE N. GORDON

COMMON WISDOM (or ignorance), as manifest in most communication text books, places the origins of propaganda in the middle of the Reformation and associates them with the Vatican's College to propagate the faith in face of galloping heresies of the seventeenth century. This is sheer philology, although most media mystics do not know it. Obviously, they think, modern propaganda techniques are an outgrowth of print technology, growing literacy rates in Europe and all the other trappings of what they like to call the "print tradition." This fits neatly into their scenario of the mythical transition from oral to written to electric cultures, or however they choose to re-define history.

Nonsense this is, in the most polite construction of the term, and nonsense it forever remains. True enough, the word "propaganda" probably made a delayed entrance from Latin into English (and French, Spanish, Italian and German) at about this late date. But Jacques Ellul, among others, is less interested in philology than intellectual history. He locates the origins of modern propaganda in the reign of Pisistratus in the sixth century B.C., probably because the recorded history of modern political tyranny of demogogy starts here.[1] We simply do not know enough about methods of social control employed by the Egyptians (particularly Rameses II) to use the term with any assurance in reference to prior cultures. If we did, I am certain Professor Ellul would have noticed.

By the fourth century B.C. propaganda had become an ancient art in Athens, even if the Greeks chose to call it "persuasion" or some other benign term, or to subsume its functions to narrative discourse, poetry (drama to us), rhetoric, or the art of soothsaying.

This matter is not merely one of semantics. I agree that precise definitions of propaganda are not only difficult to accomplish, but they have, since the age of Hitler, become nearly impossible in the West. Propaganda, however, may be regarded simply a class of persuasion wherein emphasis is weighted far more heavily upon ends than upon means, and criteria of success depend upon results rather than qualities or processes. Calling it "organized persuasion" or "the engineering of consent" (in the manner of E. Bernays) may help to clarify for some of us this ratio of methods to outcomes. But most contemporary definitions of the term are persuasive devices themselves, either in style or intent, and belabor the obvious.

In these terms, then, Plato's literary character, Socrates was a propagandist. He was more scrupulous about his manner of discourse than many who followed him, but, particularly in the political thrust of *The Republic*, the dialogues were meticulously written to defend persuasively the master's conclusions in a canny manner that belies the time-honored mystique surrounding the ideal of Socratic dialogical education. They also merit careful comparison with other political conversations between mentor and students—say the Watergate tapes—to the degree that they cleverly explore possible options for conclusion, and then settle exactly where they were supposed to in the first place. Magnificent conversation indeed (Plato not Watergate!), but propagandistic in tenor and method.

Aristotle is in some ways more difficult to call a propagandist than Plato, just as it is harder even today to calculate the exact ratio of ends to means in the output of most realists than that of idealists. So enormous and formidable is Aristotle's extant output, however, and so human his inclination towards manipulation, particularly in political matters, that he veers frequently from his genius for keen empiricism into the role of persuader. From here it is but one step into the role of propagandist, a step, if one is to believe Ellul, that is nearly irresistible for all social observers in the transmission of the best thinking of their day.

What Aristotle was concerned with mostly—and I am here confining my observations mostly to the *Rhetoric* and incidentally to the *Poetics* [2]—was naturally persuasive methodology, displaying an acute sensitivity to techniques of communication that in breadth and clarity are seldom found in most contemporary literature on attitude change and persuasion, and with a sophistication that is deceptively modern.

Aristotle's dissection of persuasive rhetoric is, of course, an extension of his discourse on *Logic*, both a tract and a method that did not preclude persuasive motivations and that still maintains an iron hand on the study of much philosophy and all political disciplines taught in the West. Just as the *syllogism* is the building block of Aristolian logic, so the *enthymeme* is the persuasive module around which rhetoric, argumentation and propaganda are built: the "mode of persuasion" in Aristotle's words. That contemporary propaganda analysis lacks such a fundamental heuristic tool as the enthymeme seems strange, reflective only of the rigor that we still apply to logical discourse as opposed to the fragmentation of our contemporary psychologies, into which categories we have placed persuasive art. (Logic, incidentally, is no less an art than rhetoric to Aristotle.)

What, substantially, is the enthymeme of Aristotle? He quite clearly explains that it is a *pseudo*-syllogism, exactly what any modern persuasive gambit is—for instance, the copy in an advertisement for a common cold remedy that causes one to smile because of the cleverness rather than the intrinsic reasonableness of its "pitch." Such prose almost proves its point, and may to some people, but it does not jibe entirely with common sense and hardly at all with uncommon sense. And yet one cossets the feeling that the damn remedy may just be worth trying! One does not need to be a specialist at the persuasive arts to glean the enthymeme that glitter forth from the following golden prose:

> 6 or 3 or 1. Your choice. Six cold tablets, or three ounces of liquid, or just one Contac.
>
> Sneezing, drips, congestion. You've got the common cold. You want to keep medication working in your system up to 12 continuous hours.
>
> You'd need six cold tablets (two evey four hours) or three ounces of the cold liquid (one every four hours) or just one Contac.
>
> For aches, coughs and fever, the others contain things not found in Contac. Your cold. Your choice.
>
> Give your cold to Contac.

Logical? Granting certain assumptions, the pitch *nearly* yields to syllogistic reasoning, except possibly that ambiguous sentence about " . . . things not found in Contac." Persuasive? The enthymeme, that is the sense of the argument, is meaningful to those with faith that modern medicine has conquered all things, and really claims little more than that one Contac pill is as effective as six aspirin tablets or three jiggers of kickapoo juice, which is probably and unfortunately true.

The most infuriating aspect of such persuasion is that it works, precisely because of the skill with which enthymeme is used and the credulity with which it is often accepted. Aristotle explains this. "It follows plainly, therefore, that he who is best able to see how and from what elements a syllogism is produced will also be best skilled in the enthymeme . . . The true and the approximately true are apprehended by the same faculty; it may also be noted that men have a sufficient natural instinct for what is true, and usually do arrive at the truth. Hence, the man who makes a good guess at the truth is likely to make a good guess at probabilities."[3]

To the modern ear, this is shady morality, the objective of the mode of persuasion being "to discover the means of coming as near such success as the circumstances of each particular case allow," in Aristotle's words. All cozy enough when considering cold remedies, which probably murder only the vulnerable. But, notes Aristotle, "A man can confer the greatest of benefits by the right use of these (enthymemes), and inflict the greatest of injuries by using them wrongly."[4] Mindful of this *caveat*, he notes, "Rhetoric may be defined as the faculty of observing in any given case the *available means of persuasion.*"[5]

Use and control of the enthymeme is not as easy as it seems at first blush. Aristotle provides countless illustrations from Athenian culture, some of which still apply, and all of which are more easily overlooked than artfully used: political persuasion may employ any construction of a possible future time that it requires; self-interest lies at the heart of persuasive appeals to maintain the *status quo*; people should be praised for being who they are rather than what they do or do not do; when one discredits the source of a counter-argument, he discredits the argument. Examples are numerous and impressive and are more sagely recounted by Aristotle than by me.

The modern analyst of persuasion has apparently lost such control of the enthymeme as an analytic instrument by virtue of his obsession with the psychological and sociological speculation that characterizes so much contemporary propaganda analysis rather than with those elements of it that are simply (nearly) logical on their face as rhetoric in Aristotle's sense. We have lost command of the enthymeme, the fundamental module of persuasion, because we are less interested in the matters of truth than the soothingly clever detective work involved in obtuse searches for motivations. Hence, the erudite and cunning work of men like Ellul, who serve us well as historians of propaganda but never seem to provide a clear definition of exactly what persuasive discourse *is*. Because he follows his inquiries to their fount, Aristotle is not distracted from trees to forests, as most of us who claim expertise in the analysis of persuasion are forced to be in an era in which scientific psycho- and socio-logic have replaced, since the end of Age of Reason, much of our faith in the logic of language.

Some "content analysis" projects attempted in recent years, have, know it or not, groped after the concept of the enthymeme with some little success, because enthymemes are, as Aristotle notes, less easily quantified than qualified, at least when compared to syllogisms. Yet, the contemporary propagandist (and his Boswells) often works with enthymemes in much the way that Aristotle describes them, rather like the man who was speaking prose all his life and did not know it. To call, as the editor of my edition of the *Rhetoric* does, an enthymeme a "rhetorical argument" is all right as far as it goes, but such a superficial translation leaves much for Aristotle to explain.

He is brief and quite specific,[6] severing what he calls "non-essentials" in rhetorical persuasion from what lies at its heart. These non-essentials are emotional and theatrical matters, admittedly related to effective persuasion but not at its core. While we emphasize today such devices as appeals to "prejudice, pity and similar emotions," in Aristotle's words as essential *devices* of propaganda, Aristotle would disagree (and rightly so, I think) with the worship of them in our modern textbooks, because they are evasions from the two central points of persuasive discourse: *its topic and relevance to the lives of those who are exposed to it*. Here is the enthymeme exposed—what Aristotle calls the "demonstrations," that is, *what* is said or done to achieve the desired persuasive outcome that, in the end, determines the right *way* in which it is done if it is to accomplish its end. Aristotle, accordingly, avoids tiresome moral discussions about differing emphases upon the ethics of ends and means in much the same way that similar arguments are irrelevant to his logic. *What* is *done* in persuasive matters is the essential point; *how* it is done is equivocal and variable, interesting but not of prior interest. The gods of intellect are therefore appeased by Aristotle's recognition that the enthymeme may (or may not) depend upon syllogistic reasoning—or the ability to accomplish it—but does not necessarily need to be logical in a *mathematical* sense, merely demonstrable in what we would call today a "legal" sense, in the broadest construction of the latter term, like our cold remedy advertisement that is indeed legal.

The modern student of propaganda, naturally, senses the presence of the dominance of the enthymeme but does not quite know why. He would rather equivocate by means of psychoanalytic ephemera or psychological hypotheses than face the issue (or fact) of the enthymeme. Hitler's notion of the "big lie" is, of course, a repellent notion to any admirer of human rationality, but it also is, nevertheless, given grudging recognition as a quasi-truth in the annals of contemporary propaganda analysis, hedged in by irrelevant qualifications and voluntaristic thinking. If one reduces the grandiose boast of the "big lie" to an enthymeme, the matter is not only clear, it is explicable and intensely rational. First, as a generalization it is on its face an absurd construct. Second, *what* big lie are we talking about, proposed by whom and addressed to whom? If we mean the German Fuehrer's *specific* notion that the Jews were sub-human social parasites, and if we examine the social, political and psychological climate into which his madness spilled in the 1930s, the demonstrable nature of Hitler's argument *in that time and place for the ears that listened to it* is both lucidly and tragically apparent. It qualifies as an Aristotelian enthymeme, not simply because of its persuasive success as history but because of its capacity for demonstration. Much of Hitler's propaganda and its surface absurdity might not have been laughed at abroad for so long if it had been recognized for what it was before it was too late. History, however, also tells us that not all big lies produce viable enthymemes for all publics—that is, some are demonstrable and some are not.

Aristotle sees the enthymeme as the equivalent in rhetoric to the syllogism in logic, but the matter does not end there. Granting the enthymeme's place at the heart of persuasion, Aristotle is also concerned with "nonessentials" in rhetoric. These are, in modern terms, the media by which enthymemes are fused into the minds of publics. To this end, a wide and variegated lexicon of metaphor is drawn up for analysis. It centers upon the use of languge but, in main thrust, it is concerned with the categorization of symbolic words and phrases that relate the objectives of propaganda to the emotional concerns of the people to whom it is addressed. Such metaphorical analysis reaches its literary apogee in the *Poetics*, but the power of such elaboration of enthymemes is candidly discussed in the *Rhetoric* both extensively and cleverly.

Where both essays overlap most noticeably is in the role of *character* in persuasive discourse. The convergence is inevitable, because the spine of all communication is imitation (called "emulation" in the *Rhetoric*) of one form or another. Propaganda and persuasion are therefore close relatives of the ultimate form of imitation: theatre. Aristotle has drawn up an extensive *dramatis personae* in the *Rhetoric* who function in two major domains, both dramatistic and hence persuasive. On one hand, there are *real* characters, most notably the progagandist (or advocate and his client if he has one) and the audience that he is addressing. On the other, the world of metaphors is peopled by symbolic characters—good men, bad men, jealous lovers, thieves, drunkards and fools— who serve as vehicles through which enthymemes are demonstrated and by means of which both the minds and the emotions of the public are activated. In this theater of imaginary contemporaries (and real ones and characters from Homer and the tragic and comic theatrical repertoire of Aristotle's day, some still powerfully familiar), Aristotle develops a vocabulary of symbolic performers who, in effect, deliver his enthymemes in the timeless quick-sketch methods of the dramatist, ancient and modern, to activate quite specifically the thoughts and feelings of his auditors.

Our modern political manipulators talk today of "images" and "image candidates," as if their persuasive magic was generated by the television tube. Aristotle the propagandist is competent to conjure, even for the modern reader, enough potent images of characters—some of them politicians—to feed an advertising agency for decades, with an uncanny ability that locates precisely those specific traits of behavior that exemplify the demonstration of the enthymeme and the objective of his persuasion. One feels that such virtuosity is as unfair to the *Logos* of the ancient world as our "image candidates" are to that of the modern one. But it is one measure of the liberal thrust of Aristotle's intellect that he finds no dissonance in the ruthless exercise of his talent as a dramatist with that of a logician, a confidence to ponder in this age of faith in science.

If the basic unit of the propagandist's art is the enthymeme, its main medium of discourse is the persuasive power of the personalities that inhabit its symbols, rituals, and its world of metaphors. Given what Aristotle calls the "proof" of the argument (real or apparent), and the game plans by which one unfolds it, a near automatic machine is set in motion that steers inexorably towards the propagandist's objective. By no means will he necessarily moderate attitudes in modern terms, or win his case in ancient ones, but he will have followed both the ancient and modern paradigm of those propagandists who, in whatever terms they judge it, achieve success. The technology that is brought to bear upon this process will, of course, constitute a function of the "time frame," in today's parlance, in which it is attempted. But cameras and microphones and printing presses have little to do with the matter: process is all.

In fact, both Hitler and Lenin at one or another time proposed one particular hypothesis that is distinctively Aristotelian and yet quite relevant to modernity: that the living, spoken word is a better vehicle for persuasion than print, recordings or simulations of any type. I hope they are wrong, simply because nearly everybody today believes they *are*, thus making available a potentially powerful weapon for the intelligent tyrant who might capitalize upon what we believe to be our invulnerability to mere words and clever speakers who shun the mass media.

Aristotle would have known what to do about this problem—of this I am certain. I do not.

NOTES AND REFERENCES

[1] Jacques Ellul, *Histoire de la Propagande* (Paris: *Presses Universitaires de France*, 1967), pp. 8–11.

[2] The edition of these works used here is *Rhetoric*, translated by W. Rhys Roberts and *Poetics*, translated by Ingram Bywater (New York: The Modern Library, 1954), to which all references below refer.

[3] *Rhetoric*, Book III, Chapter 2, p. 22.

[4] *Ibid.*, p. 23.

[5] *Ibid.*, p. 24. Italics added.

[6] *Ibid.*, Book 1, Chapter 1, pp. 19–22.

DAVID HARVEY was born in Bideford, Devon, England in 1937. He was educated at Blundell's School, Tiverton and Oriel College, Oxford. In 1964 he married Hazel van Rest; they have two children, a son and a daughter.

Mr. Harvey has been a lecturer in the Department of Classics at the University of Exeter since 1962. In 1967–8 he was Junior Research Fellow at the Center for Hellenic Studies at Washington, D.C. He has been a member of the Council of the Society for the Promotion of Hellenic Studies, and is Secretary of the South-West branch of the Classical Association.

He has published articles on Greek history and Greek political thought in the *Revue des Études Grecques*, the *Journal of Hellenic Studies*, *Historia*, *Classica et Mediaevalia* and other journals; of these his article "Literacy in the Athenian Democracy" (*R.E.G.* 79 (1966)) is most relevant to the theme of this volume. A joint translation of Karl Reinhardt's book *Sophokles* by Hazel and David Harvey will be published by Blackwell's of Oxford in 1978.

Greeks and Romans Learn to Write[1]

by F. DAVID HARVEY

For Bernard Knox on his sixtieth birthday

T HERE ARE two kinds of communication, verbal and non-verbal; and there are two kinds of verbal communication, spoken and written. The skill of speaking is comparatively easily transmitted, for the child simply imitates those around him; but the skill of writing is more sophisticated and more difficult to transmit, and there is more than one way of doing it.[2] The purpose of this paper is to examine what is known of the methods by which writing was taught in the two great societies of the ancient world, at Athens and in Rome. A third section contains a few remarks on teaching aids, for light relief. The discussion

63

will concentrate on the *literary* evidence, which in my view has often been mishandled and confused. Very little will be said about the papyrological and epigraphic evidence, which is comparatively straightforward.

Before we look at the evidence in detail, there is one general point of some importance that should be emphasized: throughout antiquity, in both the Greek and the Roman world, learning to write (which went hand in hand with learning to read) was not a single undifferentiated experience, but a process in which there were four clearly defined stages: the first stage was to learn the letters of the alphabet; then came syllables; then words, starting with monosyllables and working up to polysyllables; and finally, the fourth stage, sentences, usually lines of poetry.[3] This progression is succinctly described by St. Jerome,[4] who marks off the stages as follows: "she should get to know her alphabet, join syllables, learn names (or nouns), and put words together in sentences." Modern scholars who have discussed individual passages of our literary texts have often lost sight of this fundamental point, and the result has been a number of muddles—for instance, as we shall see, there has been a misguided attempt to interpret a Greek account of stage four by comparing it with Roman accounts of stage one; and if this paper does no more than straighten out some of these muddles, it will have served its purpose.

GREECE

There is only one passage in classical Greek literature which gives us detailed information about the way in which children were taught to write. The passage comes in the course of a speech which Plato puts into the mouth of the sophist Protagoras in his dialogue of that name (326 c–e). The dialogue was probably written in the 390s B.C., and the action is envisaged as taking place in the late 430s, just before the outbreak of the Peloponnesian war. The passage runs as follows: "When they have done with masters, the state again compels them to learn the laws and live after the pattern which they furnish, and not after their own fancies; and just as in learning to write the writing-master first draws lines (*hypograpsantes grammas*) with a stilus for the use of the young beginner, and gives him the tablet and makes him draw according to the guidance of the lines (*graphein kata tēn hyphēgēsin tōn grammōn*), so the city draws the laws, which were the invention of good lawgivers living in the olden time, and compels the young man to rule and be ruled in accordance with them. He who transgresses them is to be corrected, or, in other words, require to put his account straight (*euthynai*), which is a term used not only in your country but also in many others, seeing that justice puts men straight."[5]

Plato uses the teaching method as a simile, on the assumption that his readers will be familiar with the process and will fill in the details for themselves; and it is precisely because of this assumption that two quite different interpretations have been proposed.

Does Plato mean that the master traced the outlines of the "letters" (*grammas*) on a writing-tablet with his stilus, and that the pupil then filled them in? This view is argued for at some length in the commentary of J. and A.M. Adam;[6] and since this is the commentary most commonly used by English-speaking readers of the *Protagoras*, their interpretation has become the traditional one. Moreover, the simple diagram offered by the Adams helps to imprint their view on the memory of those who use the commentary. The diagram may be compared to a Polo mint or Lifesaver on the left, representing the master's outline of omicron, and a somewhat emaciated doughnut on the right, representing the outline as filled in by the pupil. It is this interpretation which has found its way into the relevant entries in Liddell and Scott's Greek lexicon, and it is found in the standard history of ancient education, that of Marrou.[7] Neither in Liddell and Scott nor in Marrou is there the slightest hint that there might be any other explanation of the passage.

Professor E.G. Turner, however, in a recent article,[8] has argued that this interpretation should be abandoned. The *grammas* which the master draws with a stilus on the writing-tablet, he argues, are not the outlines of "letters," but parallel "lines," between which the pupil must copy the example written by the master. This teaching method is illustrated by finds from Hellenistic and Roman Egypt. Turner's interpretation had already been implied in the sixteenth century by Stephanus, argued for in the early nineteenth century by Heindorf, and adopted later in the nineteenth century by H. Sauppe;[9] but it was firmly rejected by the Adams, and has only recently been revived by Turner.

There is one significant difference between the traditional view and the parallel-lines view which has not, to the best of my knowledge, been made explicit: the traditional view rests on the assumption that Plato is talking about what I earlier called stage one, learning to write individual letters, whereas in Turner's view Plato is talking about stage four, the copying of whole sentences. This is a difference of some importance.

I am convinced that Turner is right; but his article is brief, and he makes no attempt to refute the arguments for the traditional view, as set out in the Adams' commentary; and at first sight these look impressive. It will therefore be necessary to dismantle them. The question is essentially linguistic, or rather lexical, and hinges in the first place on the interpretation of the word *grammē*.

The teachers "draw *grammas*." As Turner points out, *grammē* means a line, not a letter; what the teacher draws are therefore lines, between which the pupil must keep his writing. The Greek for "letters" is *grammata*, and if Plato had meant letters, that is the word which he should have used. The Adams circumnavigate this point by translating *grammai* as "the lines which form letters."[10] But if Plato had meant "the lines which form letters," would he really have written *grammai* rather than *grammata*? This sounds like an evasion.

Some lines are straight; some are not. The word "line" by itself may imply straightness, or it may not. But if it could be established that Plato consistently uses the word *grammē* to mean a straight line, the traditional interpretation would be impossible: for how could a teacher write the outline of theta or phi or, for that matter, the Adams' own example, omicron, with straight lines?

Plato uses the word *grammē* fourteen times [11] in his dialogue the *Meno*. Here there can be no doubt that he always means a straight line, or the straight side of a figure, since the dialogue is concerned at this point (the questioning of the slave) with geometrical figures based on the square. The lines that form these figures are vertical, horizontal and diagonal, but they are always straight. [12]

The word occurs twice in the *Republic*. It is first used of the notorious Divided Line (509 d) in a passage that has provoked an enormous amount of discussion; but no-one has ever suggested that the line is anything other than straight. In this context a curved, wriggly, crooked or bent line would be non-sensical. The other example in the *Republic* (534 d) is rather different: children are compared to "irrational quantities" (*alogoi grammai*), i.e. quantities incommensurable with whole numbers. But the irrational quantity *par excellence*, the one which first puzzled Greek mathematicians, is the relationship between the diagonal and the side of a square. In other words, the question of irrational quantities arose from the relationship between two straight lines, and this usage of *grammē* may be taken as an extension of the basic meaning "straight line." [13]

This leaves two examples in the *Theaetetus*. At 148 a we are still in the realm of incommensurables, and the word certainly means "straight line." At 181 a, the context is quite different: "as in that game they play in the wrestling-schools, where the players are caught by both sides and dragged both ways at once across the line (*dia grammēs*)." The game is a variety of tug-of-war (*diel-kystinda* cf. Pollux 9.112), and the line will have been straight.

The result of this inquiry, then, is that in every case except one where Plato uses the word *grammē* he means a straight line, and even the exception is derived from the same meaning. Moreover, it is significant that Plato never feels the need to add the word "straight." It is therefore overwhelmingly probable that *grammē* in the Protagoras passage means a *straight* line; this is entirely consistent with the parallel-lines view, and it makes the traditional view untenable. To clinch the matter, as Turner says, the last sentence of the passage from the Protagoras contains a play on the meaning of the words *euthynein* and *euthynai*—difficult to reproduce in English: "put straight" is an attempt to capture it—that makes no sense unless the teacher's lines are thought of as straight.

The second word in Plato's description that we must examine is the one rendered as "draw under" (*hypographein*). The traditional view envisages the schoolmaster drawing the outlines of the letters "under" where the pupil's completed letters will eventually be, "under" in the sense that a painter's sketch lies underneath the finished work; whereas the alternative view envisages the schoolmaster drawing parallel lines under the words to be copied—"under" in the sense of further down the page as one reads.

Plato uses this verb seven more times and at first sight these instances might seem to support the traditional translation, for it is indeed applies to a painter's preliminary sketch. But let us look a little closer.

At Republic 501 a, *hypograpsasthai schēma* is used in a context which explicitly refers to a painter's outline sketch—but note the word *schēma*, "outline": the verb alone does not mean "to draw an outline under"; Plato has to use *schēma* to make his meaning clear. The same is true at 548 d (cited by the Adams): a painter's preliminary sketch, certainly, but it is the word *schēma* that does the work.

At *Theaetetus* 171 e, *hypographein* is used with *logon* to mean "the doctrine which we have sketched out." So too in the *Laws* the tyrant can change the customs of a state, "having sketched out" (*hypograpsanta*) everything by his own example (711 b), and 734 c, we find the expression "to make an outline of the laws" (*nomous hypographein*). At 803 a the shipwright as it were "draws the ship in outline" (*hypographetai schēmata*—note *schēmata* again). And finally at 934 c, the law-giver, like a painter, must "sketch out actual cases on the lines of the written law" (*hypographein erga hepomena tēi graphēi*).

In other words, the verb, when used of the preliminary sketch of the painter, whether explicitly or by implication, takes this precise meaning from its context, generally from the noun it governs. Drawing an outline is not something that can be done lower down on the page; nor does that make sense in the case of a sketch of a doctrine or laws. But if it is the context that determines the sense of the verb, then it follows that in the case of the *Protagoras* the verb must mean, exceptionally, "to draw under" in Turner's sense: for we have already seen that *grammai* must be straight lines, and when Plato writes *hypograpsantes grammas* he can hardly be talking about a "rough sketch of a straight line"—virtually a self-contradiction.

Elsewhere in Greek the verb certainly means "to draw under" or "to write under" in the sense of "further down the page." We find the Athenians "writing under" the inscription recording their treaty with Sparta that the Spartans had violated their oaths; on a fourth-century inscription instructions are given that "the names of the Akarnanians are to be written on the same stele, and the cities of Akarnania from which each comes are to be written underneath"; and we find one orator impeaching another for a decree he had proposed, "and," he says, "I wrote his decree under the impeachment." [14] It seems clear that this is the sense in which the verb is used in the *Protagoras* passage.

What finally are we to make of the phrase "draw according to the guidance (*hyphēgēsis*) of the lines"? In Plato, this is the sole occurrence of this noun, but he uses the corresponding verb *hyphēgeisthai* quite frequently, and the Adams in their commentary write of this verb that it is "similarly used"—i.e. in the same way as *hypographein*, of an outline drawing—"only with the added idea of guiding." Is this true?

Plato uses the verb fourteen times, in dialogues early, middle and late. [15] In nearly every case it means simply "to lead" or "to guide," or "to show, indicate or suggest," without any allusion whatever to outline drawing. In the one passage where the concept of an "outline" is present (*Republic* 403 e), the idea of an outline is given not by the verb but by the noun—"we will indicate the general outlines" (*typous*). One other is ambiguous, meaning either "as the law-giver indicates in the laws he writes" or "as he sketches out the laws" (*Laws* 890 c). These are the only two passages that the Adams' commentary cites; nothing is said of the numerous passages where the meaning is simply "to guide" and so forth. In the *Protagoras* passage, then, if we may infer the meaning of the noun from Plato's use of the verb, the phrase means simply "to write along the guide-lines," that is, along the parallel lines; there is no allusion to any "preliminary sketch."

We may conclude, then, that the school-master wrote the words to be copied, and then drew parallel lines underneath, between which his pupil was to copy them. This is the procedure alluded to by Plato and objections against it have no weight. If for a moment we turn our attention away from the examination of the text, and consider instead the educational efficiency of the methods envisaged by the rival interpretations, it is obvious which is the superior: copying is a sensible, intelligent method by comparison with merely filling in the teacher's outlines, a procedure which would hardly be likely to impress the shapes of the letters on the pupil's mind. Furthermore, the parallel-lines interpretation brings the passage in the *Protagoras* into agreement with another passage in which Plato speaks of learning to write, in his dialogue the *Charmides*,[16] "to write the same letters at the writing-master's house." Here Plato is thinking chiefly of the copying, and does not mention the parallel lines, whereas in the *Protagoras* he is thinking chiefly of the parallel lines, and does not mention the copying. Taken together, the two passages present the complete picture.[17] The picture is of the fourth stage: learning to copy whole sentences.

How far can we generalize from the *Protagoras* passage? Should we be cautious and simply say that this is a method by which some Greeks were taught to write; or, as Turner's title implies, the method by which Athenians were taught to write; or, more boldly, the method by which the Greeks were taught to write; or what? Consideration of modern practice would suggest that we should be cautious. In Britain, despite such unifying factors as a nation-wide state educational system, the multiplication of copies of textbooks by means of printing, and the wide use of television, the methods by which writing is taught still differ from one school to another. If this is the case today, we ought not to expect uniformity in ancient Greece, which not only lacked these unifying factors, but was an agglomeration of highly idiosyncratic city-states, each with its individual and peculiar character and institutions. However, the passage we have been discussing is part of a speech put into the mouth of Protagoras, a man from Abdera; amongst his audience are Prodicus of Ceos, Hippias of Elis, Antimoerus of Mende and, although he is speaking at Athens, more non-Athenians than Athenians (*Protagoras* 315 a–d); and it might be argued that in such a Panhellenic gathering Protagoras ought to have chosen for his simile a process with which all his audience would have been familiar. But would Plato have bothered about a detail of this kind? He occasionally mentions events in his dialogues that are anachronistic, in the sense that they are subsequent to the dramatic date;[18] and he may well have mentioned a method of teaching with which he himself was familiar without stopping to think how appropriate it would be to the dramatic context. But the fact remains that, as Turner has shown, the same method of teaching can be found in Hellenistic and Roman Egypt, several centuries later and in a context far removed from the Athens of Plato; and this firm evidence, characteristic as it is of the leisurely pace of technological innovation in the ancient world, should outweigh arguments that are based on probability. It would seem reasonable to say that the method described by Plato was widely used in the Greek world from at least the fifth century B.C. onwards, though there may have been others.

The *Protagoras* passage, as Turner observes, takes the use of parallel lines back to fifth-century Athens. The idea of copying the master's work is, of course, much older and indeed universal, because obvious. It would be interesting to know whether any Near-Eastern texts have guide-lines for the pupil, and in particular to know whether this device was familiar to the Phoenicians, as it would then be reasonable to assume that it was transmitted to the Greeks together with the alphabet; we might even imagine the first Dark Age Greek to achieve literacy doing so between guide-lines drawn for him by a Phoenician. But this would take us outside the scope of the present study.

ROME

The evidence for the Roman world is better than for the Greek. This time we have not just one literary account, but three: one in Seneca, writing in the early 60s A.D., another in Quintilian, writing a generation later, towards the end of the first century, and a third in St. Jerome, writing in the first years of the fifth century. And unlike Plato, who, as we have seen, describes only the fourth stage, Quintilian describes all the stages, Seneca and St. Jerome describe the fourth stage, and all three describe the first.

Let us begin, then, by looking at the evidence for stage one, the learning of letters. Seneca writes: "Boys learn in accordance with a written model (*praescriptum*); their fingers are held, and they are guided by the hand of another through the forms (*simulacra*) of the letters."[19] Like Plato, Seneca takes the method of learning to write and uses it for a simile, assuming that his readers will be familiar with the process. We are not; and though the general meaning is clear, the details are vague. The child holds a writing implement; the parent or master grasps his fingers from above and guides them so that he forms letters instead of the random scratches that would result if he were left on his own. (This is straightforward enough: I have seen it in my own family.) Before him is the *praescriptum*, the "written model," as I have translated it; literally, that which has been written beforehand.

But what material is the *praescriptum* written on? And what material does the child make his copy on? The answer to these questions is surely that Seneca is talking in the most general manner, and is simply not interested in these details. The model letters might be on papyrus, or on a waxed writing-tablet, or scratched on any convenient surface—or the child might take as his model any written matter that happened to come his way: in the Roman world, the inscriptions under the family portraits in the atrium, perhaps; in the modern world the back of a corn-flakes packet. The alphabets inscribed on a marble plaque found near Rome and on a tile found in Pannonia,[20] for example, may have served as *praescripta*; more frequently, no doubt, more perishable material would have been employed. If the child's writing-implement was a stilus, he will have made his copy on a waxed tablet or a slate or a tile; but Seneca does not specify a stilus, so for all we know the child may be writing on the floor or the walls or the furniture—as with the *praescriptum*, anything will have done.

It has been necessary to stress this point because it has always been assumed that the *praescriptum* must have been lightly traced on the wax surface of a writing-tablet, and that when Seneca writes "they are guided through the forms of the letters" he means that the child's fingers are guided over this "preliminary sketch" on the wax.[21] It is easy to see how this interpretation arose: *praescriptum* can be used of a painter's preliminary sketch (see e.g. Pliny, *Naturalis Historia* 35.36.92); the waxed tablet—a wooden tablet coated with wax to provide a writing-surface for the stilus—was the standard material in antiquity for any kind of writing that was not intended to be permanent; and once one knows Quintilian's views on learning to write (which we shall consider next), the temptation to read them into the Seneca passage is very strong. But Seneca's language is quite ambiguous. Boys learn *ad praescriptum*, "in accordance with that which has been written beforehand": it might have been on the wax, or it might have been elsewhere. Their fingers are guided *per litterarum simulacra*, "through the forms of the letters": the *simulacra* might have been already scratched on the wax, or they might have appeared as the child wrote. An *a priori* argument is perhaps stronger: it is unlikely that anyone would have thought of carving grooves into wood for the benefit of learners, as described in the passage of Quintilian that we shall be considering, if it had not already been done on the normal writing surface, wax. Quintilian's suggestion sounds like an improvement on a technique already in use, not a total innovation. Maybe: but if so, it proves that incision into the wax was practiced, not that Seneca had anything so specific in mind. And I see no reason to suppose that he did.

Quintilian's method, indeed, is quite different. He writes: "As soon as the child has begun to follow the outlines (*ductus*) of the letters, it will not be a bad idea to have them cut as accurately as possible on a board (*tabella*), so that the stilus may be guided through them as though through furrows. This will ensure that the stilus will make no slips, such as occur on wax tablets, since it will be confined by the edges on either side, and will be unable to stray outside the written model (*praescriptum*); and by following the firm tracks (*vestigia*) more rapidly and more frequently, he will strengthen his finger-joints; and he will not need the help of the teacher's hand placed over his to guide it."[22]

What procedure is Quintilian advocating? The letters are to be carved on a board (*tabella*). A *tabella* is a writing-tablet, made of wood; and as we have seen, such tablets were generally coated with wax. Thus *tabella* frequently means a waxed tablet, and that is how Turner takes it here: "it will be useful [for the master] to trace letters as clearly as possible *in the wax*." So too Marrou: "lettres . . . que le poinçon de l'enfant retrace en suivant le sillon *à travers la cire*" (my italics in each case).[23] But this cannot be right, since Quintilian goes on to *contrast* the method that he is recommending with writing on wax: "The stilus will make no slips, such as occur on wax tablets." His own recommendation is that the letters should be carved into an untreated wooden tablet.[24]

He adds that this method is superior to another, which involves the teacher in guiding the pupil's hand from above with his own. Quintilian's method enables the pupil to do it more often (*saepius*) because he can do it at any time, and does not have to wait until the master can spare time for him; and he can do it more quickly (*celerius*) because of the firm tracks (*certa vestigia*) on the wooden board—there is no risk of slipping out of the groove, and so the pupil need not be cautious about it, and can do his work at greater speed. Some scholars[25] have implied that Quintilian's method is the same as that mentioned by Seneca. But on the contrary, Seneca's method is the one which Quintilian rejects as inferior to his own suggestion of carving letters in wood. Quintilian's method, as he says himself, does not require the master's helping hand, whereas this is exactly what Seneca's method does involve: "their fingers are held and they are guided by the hand of another."

Other scholars[26] have taken both the Seneca passage and the Quintilian passage and have tried to use them to elucidate the passage in Plato's *Protagoras*. I need hardly say at this stage what a misguided procedure this is.

It has also been suggested[27] that bricks inscribed before firing with moral maxims, which have been found in various parts of the Roman empire, may have been used in the way that Quintilian advocates instead of wooden boards. This idea cannot be rejected as impossible; but it is important to remember that Quintilian, as the context makes clear, is talking about single letters, or stage one, as we have called it, whereas the copying of maxims comes later, at stage four—and by this time one would have thought that the pupil could dispense with grooves. They may however have served as models (*proposita*) to be copied onto a waxed tablet at that later stage.

In 400 A.D. or shortly thereafter St. Jerome wrote a letter on the subject of how a girl ought to be educated. This is what he has to say about her learning to write: "When she begins to apply the stilus to the wax tablet with her unsteady hand, either let her fingers be guided by the hand of another placed over hers, or else let the letters be cut on a board, so that the traces will be kept in by the edges and be drawn through the same furrows, and will be unable to stray outside them."[28]

Quite obviously, Jerome has the Quintilian passage at the back of his mind, to such an extent that this may be regarded as a close paraphrase of it, or even—since many of the words are identical—as a rough quotation of it from memory. The only way in which he differs from Quintilian is that he presents the two methods, wax and wood, as alternatives, whereas Quintilian had recommended the use of grooves on wooden tablets as superior to wax. It is worth noting again that the method using waxed tablets does not involve preliminary outlines—or at least, they are not mentioned; and that the grooves are again carved into the wood, not the wax. Presumably St. Jerome is describing a technique with which he himself is familiar, and not merely indulging in a literary reference; surely he would not have offered a parent advice culled from a textbook more than 300 years old if he had come across anything more up-to-date in his own experience. If so, teaching methods have not changed at all throughout these three centuries. I have already spoken of the leisurely pace of technological innovation in the ancient world; here it has simply ground to a halt.

That St. Jerome is not merely echoing Quintilian, but is indeed referring to contemporary practice, appears to be confirmed by his contemporary St. Ambrose, who says of cedar-wood: "This material is chosen for use in building the roofs of houses and in shaping the letters of the alphabet, which imbue children in their youth with the love of liberal studies."[29] This passage is unfortunately ambiguous: Ambrose might have in mind either the teaching method recommended by Quintilian, or a set of separate wooden letters (on which see below); but there are good reasons for believing that he is referring to the former.[29a]

A not altogether dissimilar device was used by at least one illiterate who needed to write—according to one chronicler, no less a figure than Theodoric the Ostrogoth, king of Italy from 493 to 526 A.D. "So ignorant did he remain of the first elements of science," writes Gibbon,[30] "that a rude mark was contrived to represent the signature of the illiterate king of Italy. The first four letters of his name (ΘΕΟΔ) were inscribed on a gold plate, and when it was fixed on the paper, the king drew his pen through the intervals." A luxury stencil, in other words. There can be little doubt, however, that Theoderic, educated as he was at the court of Constantinople, knew perfectly well how to write; it was his contemporary Justin I who was the illiterate (Procopius, *Secret History* 6. 14–16), and the name of Theoderic has at some stage been erroneously inserted into the anecdote.

So much for the first stage. After the child had learnt his letters, he moved on to stage two, syllables, and then, by joining syllables, to stage three, words. These intermediate stages are clearly described by Quintilian (1.1.30–1); they present no problems of interpretation and therefore call for no comment.

Finally, then, the pupil copies phrases written by his master. The sentence which I have already quoted from Seneca continues: "then they (the boys) are told to copy what is put in front of them and improve their handwriting by comparison with it." The same process is described by Quintilian[31] at greater length—the key phrase reads "those lines, which are put in front of children for them to write out a copy." Quintilian is anxious that these sentences should be sound moral maxims (*honestum aliquid*)—a typically Roman attitude, one would be tempted to add, if it were not that the Greeks had sometimes—though by no means always!—chosen similarly edifying maxims for copying.[32] The verbal similarity between Seneca and Quintilian here is not significant; it is simply dictated by the subject-matter.

This fourth stage, the copying of sentences, is of course identical with that described by Plato in the *Protagoras* and *Charmides*. Commentators have rightly sought to compare the method described in the *Protagoras* passage with the accounts given by Roman writers; but they have compared it with the wrong stage. Plato, as we have seen, is describing the final stage, the copying of sentences; but instead of citing the parallels from Seneca and Quintilian for this stage—the phrases that I have just quoted in the last paragraph—they have perversely cited their descriptions of the first stage, the learning of the shapes of letters.

It so happens that Seneca and Quintilian do not mention parallel lines. This is only a detail; they may well have been used,[33] but the Roman writers may not have thought it necessary to mention them. They are not relevant to the points they are making. For Plato, on the contrary, it was just this detail that he needed for his simile.

TEACHING AIDS

In this final section, I hope to enliven our picture of ancient teaching methods by discussing the literary evidence for some of the teaching aids devised by the Romans. There may well have been others.

Ivory and wooden letters

Toys in the form of letters of the alphabet are an obvious way to make learning more attractive. We first hear of them in the first century A.D., from Quintilian: 'I quite approve of a practice which has been devised to stimulate children to learn by giving them ivory letters to play with, as I do of anything else that may be discovered to delight the very young, the sight, handling and naming of which is a pleasure."[34] "Anything else that may be discovered" (*si quid aliud inveniri potest*) seems to imply that ivory letters were the only educational toys known to Quintilian.

St. Jerome says much the same: "Have a set of letters made for her, of boxwood or of ivory, and tell her their names. Let her play with them, making play a road for learning, and let her not only grasp the right order of the letters and remember their names in a song, but also frequently upset their order and mix the last letters with the middle ones, the middle with the first. Thus she will know them all by sight as well as by sound."[35] The only novelty here, apart from the song (what tune?, one wonders; perhaps no more than a chant on a monotone), is the suggestion that the toy letters might be made of boxwood instead of ivory. Ivory letters could presumably be afforded only by the wealthy upper class, to whom Quintilian addressed his work.

The context of these passages is worth noting: in both cases they come immediately before the advice on teaching children to write that has been discussed above. In other words, learning the shapes and names of the letters in this way preceded any attempt to write them.

Cakes

In the *Leabhar Breac* (the "Speckled Book"), an Irish manuscript copied in the early fifteenth century but incorporating much earlier material, there is a life of St. Columba which contains the following passage:[36] "Now, when came the time for him to read, the cleric went to a certain spaeman [i.e. soothsayer] who was biding in the country, to ask him when the boy ought to begin. When the spaeman had scanned the sky, he said 'Write for him his alphabet now.' It was therefore written on a cake, and in this wise Colombcille [Columba] ate the cake, to wit, half thereof to the east of the water and the other half to the west of the water." (This signified, as the spaeman explained, that the saint's activity was to be in both Scotland and Ireland.) "Not long thereafter," we read, the cleric, his foster-father, is overcome with shyness when he is required to sing a psalm. Columba does it for him, "and yet theretofore he had read his alphabet only." Clearly, he had absorbed his letters by eating the cake.

In a spirited article, H. Gaidoz[37] has argued that the miraculous element in this anecdote may be discounted, and that in post-Roman Ireland children were given cakes on which were inscribed the letters of the alphabet in order to encourage them to learn to read (and presumably also to write). (Modern parallels come to mind: biscuits decorated with iced letters, alphabet soup (*Nudelbuchstaben*), etc.). Gaidoz then argues that the barbarous Irish who came into contact with Romano-Christian civilization, "those mastodons at the oases of *litterae humaniores*," were incapable of inventing anything; rather, they were transmittors of Roman culture; therefore this teaching method is Roman. Admittedly there is no evidence, but there is perhaps an allusion in Horace (*Satires* 1.1.25–26):

> *ut pueris olim dant crustula blandi*
> *doctores, elementa*[38] *velint ut discere prima,*

"as teachers sometimes give little cakes to boys, to coax them into wanting to learn their alphabet."

This chain of hypotheses is too tenuous to support its conclusion. Scholarly caution should make us hesitate to rationalize the magic of a miracle-story into an everyday teaching method. It is unreasonable to insist that a detail of a medieval Irish tale must be derived from Roman practice. And the quotation from Horace is irrelevant: it has nothing to do with alphabetical cakes, but refers to what might be called the use of cakes as carrots—as incentives to learning, or rewards for progress. The same practice is referred to in the fifth century by St. Jerome, in the passage cited at the beginning of this article: "meanwhile she should get to know her alphabet, join syllables, learn names (or nouns), and put words together in sentences; and to persuade her to practise with her squeaky little voice, little honey-cakes should be placed in front of her as rewards." [39] Jerome goes on to list other such rewards: sweets, flowers, gems and dolls.

Cakes are mentioned by Marrou, [40] at first correctly as rewards; then he speaks of "cakes in the form of letters," without any clear indication of date. He refers in a note to Gaidoz' article and to a work on the medieval Talmudic schools of France; but the general context would seem to imply that they were also known in the classical period at Rome; if so, he is mistaken. He also confuses cakes with alphabets on them (as in the story of St. Columba), and cakes in the form of individual letters. The latter seem to have been invented by medieval Jewish teachers, who rewarded good pupils with spiced bread in the shape of letters of the alphabet. "Comme la Tora est douce!" exclaimed the grateful pupils. [41]

Boys

The oddest method of teaching the alphabet that we hear of in antiquity is that which is said to have been devised in the second century A.D. by the wealthy Athenian Herodes Atticus. "When his son could not master his alphabet," we read, "the idea occurred to Herodes to bring up with him twenty-four boys of the same age named after the letters of the alphabet, so that he would be obliged to learn his letters at the same time as the names of the boys." [42] How did he get hold of twenty-four boys of the same age for use as a teaching aid? The word translated "boys" (*paides*) can also mean slaves; and I suspect that that is what they were. Even in a modern school, however, the gimmick might be tried by infant teachers, if they had a class of the right number (extra pupils might be full stops, question marks, etc.)—but for the benefit of the whole group.

Tail-piece on literate elephants

In the elder Pliny's *Natural History* (8.3.6) we read: "Mucianus who was three times consul states that an elephant actually learnt the shapes of the Greek letters and used to write out in words of that language: 'I myself wrote this and dedicated these spoils won from the Celts'." The Greek has been reconstructed by the seventeenth-century scholar Hardouin in the form of a hexameter: *Autos egō tad' egrapsa, laphyra te Kelt' anethēka.* [43]

This anecdote raises all sorts of questions. What Celtic spoils? When were they dedicated? and where? Why "used to write" (*solitum*)?—surely a dedication is a single act, not one that one repeats—or is it that once the elephant had learnt to write the words there was no stopping him? Had Mucianus himself seen the creature? I do not know the answer to any of these questions. In the present context it is more interesting to consider whether the story is credible. C. Licinius Mucianus, the author of a collection of *mirabilia* (astonishing stories), is not the most reliable of sources; it has indeed been suggested that Pliny feels it necessary to mention his three consulships to guarantee his credibility,[44] just as one might write "Mr. Nixon, twice President of the United States, asserts . . ." to guarantee the truth of what follows.

A passage of Aelian[45] gives us confidence in Mucianus' story, and enables us to guess how it was done. "And I myself," he says, "have seen an elephant actually writing Roman letters with its trunk on a tablet in a straight line without any deviation. The only thing was that the instructor's hand was laid upon it, directing it to the shape of the letters until the animal had finished writing; and it looked intently down. You would have said that the animal's eyes had been taught and knew the letters." Here is a first-hand account, which we have no reason to suspect: the instructor with his hand on the elephant's trunk presumably manipulated it. As with the schoolboys in Seneca, it was "guided by the hand of another through the forms of the letters." One is entitled to doubt whether its education progressed any further.[46]

NOTES AND REFERENCES

[1] The "preliminary sketch" for this article was completed at the Center for Hellenic Studies, Washington D.C., in 1968. I am most grateful to Professor E.G. Turner for reading the penultimate draft and making a number of suggestions, and to Dr. L. Brandwood for sending me a number of entries from his forthcoming concordance to Plato in advance of publication. Errors and eccentricities that remain are all my own.

[2] For various modern methods see W.S. Gray. *The Teaching of Reading and Writing* (Unesco and London, 1956), 188–227, esp. 218–9.

[3] I have set out the evidence for the Greek world in the *Revue des Études Grecques* 79 (1966), 631–3; for the Roman world, the most explicit source is Quintilian, *Institutio Oratoria* 1.1. 24–36; the rest of the evidence for Roman practice, which corresponds closely with Greek, is collected in H.-I. Marrou, *Histoire de l'éducation dans l'antiquité*[6] (Paris, 1965) (henceforward Marrou) 395–7 = Eng. trs. (Mentor paperback, 1964) 363–6. This "synthetic" approach is now disapproved of: Gray, op. cit., 193–4.

[4] *Letter* 128.1.4; misunderstood by the Loeb translator, who offers "she must learn her alphabet, spelling, grammar, and syntax."

[5] *Plato's Protagoras* trs. B. Jowett, revised by M. Ostwald (New York, 1956), with some slight changes.

[6] *Platonis Protagoras* (Cambridge 1893; henceforward Adam).

[7] Marrou 236 (= Eng. trs. 217). The list of those who have accepted this view might be extended indefinitely; in all honesty I should mention F.D. Harvey, op. cit. (note 3) 631.

[8] "Athenians learn to write: Plato *Protagoras* 326 d," *Bulletin of the Institute of Classical Studies* 12 (1965) 67–9 with plate V (henceforward Turner BICS). See also the same author's *Greek Papyri* (Oxford, 1968), 89 (with n. 43 on p. 182), and *Greek Manuscripts of the Ancient World* (Oxford, 1971), 3–4 and plate 4. Turner's interpretation is accepted by W.K.C. Guthrie, *A History of Greek Philosophy* III (Cambridge, 1969), 68 n. 1.

[9] See references in Turner BICS, and add II. Sauppe, *Platons ausgewählte Dialoge* II: *Protagoras*[4] (Berlin, 1884) ad loc.

[10] A translation now incorporated in Liddell and Scott s.v. *grammē*; it should be expunged.

[11] The statistics here and elsewhere, first taken from Ast's *Lexicon Platonicum*, have been checked against the entries in Dr. L. Brandwood's forthcoming Concordance.

[12] *Meno* 82 c, d, e *bis*, 83 c *bis*, d, 84 a, c, e, 85 a *bis*, b, 87 a.

[13] *grammē* may always have meant a "straight line" until Aristotle (*Met.* 1036 b 9) extended it to the meaning of a line that defines a circle.

[14] Thuc. 5.56.3; *Inscriptiones Graecae* II[2] no. 237 (337 B.C.), line 34; Hypereides 3.30.

[15] "To lead" or "to guide": *Crito* 54 e; *Gorgias* 455 d; *Lysis* 217 a; *Phaedo* 82 d; *Theaetetus* 148 d; *Epinomis* 980 c, 989 d. "To show, indicate or suggest": *Gorgias* 458 b; *Euthydemus* 278 c, 288 c; *Cratylus* 392 d; *Sophist* 227 d; *Laws* 890 c.

[16] 159 c.

[17] In my earlier article (note 3), 631–2, I wrongly presented the *Charmides* passage as referring to a method of teaching different from that described in the *Protagoras*. I also said of the well-known cup by Douris depicting a school-room scene (Berlin 2285) that the master is probably making the outlines on the wax for the pupil to follow (my p. 631, n. 11). This must be withdrawn; no doubt the master is about to write the line which the pupil is to copy. The suggestion of H.R. Immerwahr, "Some inscriptions on Attic pottery," *The James Sprunt Studies in History and Political Science* 46 (1964) p. 26, that inscriptions on the interior of a white-ground cup "first incised into the white ground and then painted over" are also reminiscent of the *Protagoras* (according to the traditional interpretation) should likewise be abandoned.

[18] See e.g. E.R. Dodds, *Plato: Gorgias* (Oxford, 1959), 17–18.

[19] *Epistulae Morales* 94.51.

[20] *Corpus Inscriptionum Latinarum* VI 6831; III p. 962, xxvii. 1.

[21] Adam 123, where Seneca's *per litterarum simulacra* and Quintilian's *per illos velut sulcos* are italicized as though identical in meaning; F.H. Colson, *M. Fabii Quintiliani Institutionis Oratoriae Liber I* (Cambridge, 1924), note on 1.1.27; F.J. Dölger, "Der erste Schreibunterricht in Trier nach einer Jugenderinnerung des Bischofs Ambrosius von Mailand," *Antike und Christentum* 3 (1932), 62–72 (henceforward Dölger) at 65–6; Marrou 236 (= Eng. trs. 217) (where the *Protagoras* and Seneca passages are taken together as evidence for practice in Hellenistic schools).

[22] 1.1.27.

[23] Turner BICS; Marrou 396 (= Eng. trs. 365).

[24] The device is similar to (though not identical with) a stencil. Quintilian refers twice elsewhere in passing to learning to write. In 5.14.31 he seems to have the method re-

commended here in mind—though the reference might be to letters scratched in wax. At 10.2.2 he is quite vague: he might be thinking of the model, or of letters scratched in wax, or of the method he recommends.

[25] Adam 123, explicitly; Turner BICS, implicitly.

[26] Adam 122–3; Dölger 65; Marrou 236 (= Eng. trs. 217);etc.

[27] H. Thédenat, *Bulletin de la Société nationale des Antiquités* 44 (1883), 139–42.

[28] Letter 107.4.3.

[29] *Expositio Psalmi CXVIII* 22.38.

[29] a See Dölger, esp. 63 and 71.

[30] *Decline and Fall of the Roman Empire*, (ed. Bury) vol. 4, ch. 39, 183 with n. 4 but see W. Ensslin, "Rex Theodericus inlitteratur?", *Historisches Jahrbuch* 60 (1940), 391–6.

[31] 1.1.34–6.

[32] For such *gnōmai* or *sententiae* see, for the Greek world: Marrou 237 with n. 8 on 560–1 (= Eng. trs. 217–8 with n. 8 on 520–1, plus new material); Turner BICS ad fin.; for the Roman world: Marrou 395 with n. 12 on 599 (= Eng. trs. 364 with n. 12 on 556); add Seneca, *Epistulae Morales* 94.9; *Corpus Inscriptionum Latinarum* III p. 962, xxvii. 2.

[33] Examples from Egypt cited by Turner BICS include some from the Roman period.

[34] 1.1.26 (Loeb translation).

[35] Letter 107.4.2 (Loeb transl.); *buxus* or *buxum* came to mean "writing tablet": Dölger 66–71; P. Arns, *La Technique du Livre d'après Saint Jérôme* (Paris, 1953) 29–32. For disturbing the order of the Greek alphabet, cf. St. Jerome, *Commentary on Jeremiah* 25.26 (*Patrologia Latina* vol. 24, 838 D).

[36] W. Stokes, ed. and trs., *Three Middle-Irish Homilies* (Calcutta, 1877), 103; Irish text on 102. (Alternative orthography: *Lebar Brecc*.)

[37] H. Gaidoz, "Les Gâteaux alphabétiques," *Mélanges Renier* (Bibliothèque de l,École des Hautes Études, vol. 73, 1887), 1–8.

[38] Gaidoz (op. cit. 6 n. 1) refers to the ingenious theory that the word *elementa* is derived from LMN, the first letters of the second half of the alphabet; cf. our "ABC" and "alphabet" itself (alpha-beta). Untenable, alas: see A. Walde, *Lateinisches Etymologisches Wörterbuch*[3] revised by J.B. Hofmann, I (Heidelberg, 1938) 397–8.

[39] Jerome writes *elementa, crustula* and (in the clause following that quoted) *blanditur*; Horace had written *elementa, crustula, blandi*. Perhaps Jerome had the lines of Horace in mind.

[40] P. 398 and n. 15 on 600 (= Eng. trs. 367 and n. 15 on 557).

[41] T. Perlow, *L'éducation et l'enseignement chez les Juifs* (Paris, 1931), 47 n. 3.

[42] Philostratus *Vitae Sophistarum* 558 (Loeb trans.)

[43] Loeb translation. The Greek hexameter is cited in the Budé edition by A. Ernout (1952), 109.

[44] See H. Peter, *Historicorum Romanorum Reliquiae* II (Leipzig, 1906), CXXXX–CXXXXII and especially CXXXXII; the fragments are collected on 101–7.

[45] *De Natura Animalium* 2.11 ad fin. (Loeb trans.).

[46] This article has been slightly abridged by Professor E. A. Havelock. I am grateful to him for the skilful and painless way in which the extractions have been made.

JACKSON HERSHBELL is Professor of Classics and Humanities at the University of Minnesota. Born 1935 in "Pennsylvania Dutch" country, he attended Lafayette College, Easton, Pa., and the University of Pennsylvania. From 1956–60, he was a teaching fellow at Harvard University, and worked closely with the late Raphael Demos. Eric Havelock, then Chairman of Classics, inspired him to study the Presocratics, and under Havelock's direction he wrote his Ph. D. thesis on Parmenides. In 1960 he left Harvard to attend The General Theological Seminary (Episcopal) in New York City. Ordained to the Episcopal (Anglican) Priesthod in 1964, he spent several years in a parish before going to the University of North Dakota, Grand Forks, as director of an incipient Humanities Program. In 1969–70 he was a research fellow at the Institute for Research in the Humanities, University of Wisconsin, Madison. In 1971 he came to Minnesota, and in 1977–78 was an Alexander von Humboldt Fellow at the University of Munich.

He has published numerous articles and reviews on Greek philosophy, literature and history, which have appeared in such periodicals as the *American Journal of Philology, Greek, Roman, and Byzantine Studies, Phoenix, Phronesis, Hermes,* the *Classical Journal* and the *Library Journal.* He is presently working on Plutarch as a source for the Presocratics.

The Ancient Telegraph:
War and Literacy

by JACKSON P. HERSHBELL

STUDIES OF the ancient telegraph have usually focussed on its history and technical aspects without much attention to its overall importance in understanding ancient culture and society.[1] Two features, in particular, deserve further consideration: first, the use of the telegraph for military purposes; second, the connection between the telegraph's development and the rise and spread of literacy. The present study will examine these two aspects of ancient telegraphing with the purpose of gaining more insight into the relations that existed between society and technology in the Greek and Roman worlds.

81

The close connection between telegraphing and war in the Greek world is readily documented. The fullest extant account of telegraphing in chaps. 45–47 of Bk. X of Polybius' histories, is in the context of the military campaign of Philip V of Macedon in 207 B.C. when he was opposed by the Aetolians on one side, and the Romans and Attalus in the Aegean on the other. Polybius prefaces his discussion with the following remark:

> I think that as regards the system of signalling by fire (*pyresia*) which is now of the greatest possible service in war, but was formerly undeveloped, it will be of use not to pass it over, but to give it a proper discussion.[2]

Nothing in Polybius' treatment of fire signalling suggests that it was used for anything other than military purposes. In fact, he refers to an earlier work by Aeneas, surnamed Tacitus or Poliorceticus, probably of the 4th cent. B.C., on strategy. This same Aeneas wrote other treatises on military science dealing with such topics as military preparations and the defense of fortified positions.[3]

A survey, moreover, of what is known of fire-signalling in the Greek world prior to Polybius, e.g. Homer's *Iliad*, 18.207 f., Herodotus 7. 182 and 9. 3, Thucydides 2. 94, 3. 22 and 80, 4.42 and 111, 8.102, and Xenophon *Hellen.* 6. 2, suggests that the device was used mainly, if not exclusively, in time of war or for military purposes. Even the famous beacon light of Aeschylus' *Agamemnon* was employed primarily in conjuction with a military campaign, for the play opens with the soliloquy of the watchman on the palace roof, waiting to "read the meaning in that beacon light, a blaze of fire to carry out of Troy the rumor and outcry of its capture" (*Ag.* 9–10). A later mention of signal fires in Aristophanes' comedy, *The Birds* (1161), is in connection with the guard and patrol of the newly founded city of Cloud-Cuckoo-Land.[4] Lastly, the mythical origins of fire signals or beacon lights (*pyrsoi*) confirm their military use. For according to one tradition, they were invented by Palamedes who was unjustly accused of treason to the Achaeans during the Trojan War (Hyg. *Fab.* 105), and his father, Nauplius, took vengenance on his son's execution by using Palamedes' invention: on hearing of the Achaean armada's return from Troy, Nauplius went to Euboea and during a great storm kindled beacon fires along the dangerous coast, thus luring to death many returning Achaeans. Another tradition attributes the invention of beacon lights to the Greek, Sinon, who gave the signal from the Acropolis of Troy to Agamemnon at Tenedos, that all was ready for opening the wooden horse and the approach of the Greek fleet.[5]

From some of the preserved material, of course, e.g. the *Agamemnon* and the Nauplius myth, it could be inferred that signal fires were used for peaceful means, e.g. to give messages of victory or to guide sailors to shore. But nothing in extant early Greek literature suggests any widespread use of fire signals for commerical, diplomatic, or ordinary peacetime purposes. All references to such signals seem to be found in the context of war or military activities, and according to the old Megarian Theognis, the beacon light is "the voiceless messenger of tearful war (513).

In the Roman world, the evidence for the use of fire signals for military purposes, especially the giving of alarms, is perhaps even more clear than in the Greek world. For if Riepl is correct, there is only one example in the whole of Roman history ("in der ganzen römischen Geschichte") when a fire signal was used for conveying news, namely, the signal for the fall of Sejanus which was to be relayed from Rome to the emperor Tiberius on the island of Capri.[6] According to Suetonius,

> . . . he (Tiberius) complained that he was a poor, lonely old man whom Sejanus was plotting to assassinate. But he had taken precautions against the revolt which he feared might yet break out, by ordering that his grandson Drusus, who was still alive, should be released if necessary from his prison at Rome and appointed commander-in-chief. He thought, indeed, of taking refuge at the headquarters of some provincial army and had a naval flotilla standing by to carry him off the island; where he waited on a cliff top for the distant bonfire signals (announcing all possible eventualities), which he had ordered to be sent in case his couriers might be delayed. Even when Sejanus' conspiracy had been suffocated Tiberius did not show the least sign of increased confidence, but remained in the so-called Villa Io for the next nine months.[7]

The signals mentioned above were, of course, for the emperor's private use, and were to be employed only if his couriers were delayed. Other references to fire signals in Roman literature, e.g. Livy and Caesar, all point to military and not to commercial, diplomatic, or peaceful purposes.

In view of the evidence from the Greek and Roman worlds, it is thus probably not accidental that a great scholar of classical antiquity, Hermann Diels, concluded his study of "Antike Telegraphie" in 1920 with the following observation:

> this set-up (*Einrichtung*) thoroughly withstood the test among our troops in the World War; indeed, it was developed near the War's end by means of further devices which remain secret. Thus the very latest (*Allerneuestes*) is curiously bound up with the remotest past (*allerfernste Vergangenheit*), and proves the unity of human cultural development (*die Einheit der menschlichen Kulturentwicklung*) which can be occasionally interrupted, but never totally obliterated.[8]

It should be noted that Diels is not thinking here of the electric telegraph of modern times, but of the ancient optical telegraph. Nor should his remarks be construed as those of a German warmonger, for two recent studies of ancient technology and war seem to confirm the often bellicose use of what technology there was in the ancient world.

In his study of ancient technology and society, H.W. Pleket covers many technological aspects, and it is apparent that several of these were connected with war. The sympathizers of Archytas of Tarentum, for example, helped Dionysus of Syracuse to design ballistic missiles, and under his impetus there were a number of inventions at the beginning of the 4th cent. B.C., e.g. the catapult "and numerous projectiles and strange machines of war capable of performing great services" (Diod. XIV. 41, 1–2). It was also under Dionysus that the manufacture of weapons became a state business, and the professional army came into existence. And it was in the 4th cent. that tactics were reduced to a science and became the subject of special treatises such as those of Aeneas Tacitus.[9]

Y. Garlan has also noted that war sometimes caused the ancients to exceed the natural limits of their economy, and often stimulated rapid and spectacular development in technology in

> . . . a world in prey to a kind of technological block. . . . It required the challenge of external danger to liberate man's inventive genius from the constricting prejudices against technological progress . . . the very existence of the community had to be at stake.[10]

Garlan's observations are certainly applicable to the ancient telegraph's development. For what was originally a simple device of using beacon fires, flaming torches or piles of burning wood, to signal what had been agreed on before hand, e.g. "Troy has fallen" or a "fleet has arrived at Chalcis," became by the time of Aeneas and Polybius a means of communicating not only what had happened, but what is happening. And so, if used skillfully, fire signals could be used to transmit information from a distance of several days of journey. Polybius himself provides the evidence for the development of beacon lights:

> It is evident to all in every matter, and especially in warfare, the power of acting at the right time contributes much to the success of enterprises, and fire signals are most efficient of all the devices which aid us to do this. . . . Now in former times, as fire-signals were simple beacons, they were for the most part of little use to those who used them. For the service should have been performed by signals previously determined upon, and as facts are indefinite, most of them defied communication by fire signals. . . . For it is quite impossible to have a preconcerted code for things which there was no means of foretelling.

Polybius proceeds to describe Aeneas' invention which made an advance on the previous system. It is as follows. Take two earthen vessels of exactly the same size, four and a half feet high and one and a half in diameter. Fit flat corks in these so that they slip easily up and down, and in the center of each cork fix a rod divided into equal sections of three fingers' breadth, each section clearly marked off from the next. In each space write one of the events mostly likely to occur in war, e.g. "cavalry arrived in the country," "heavy infantry," or "infantry and cavalry," etc. until all the spaces are filled. Then tap the vessels carefully near the bottom with holes of the same size, so the same amount of water will run from each tap within a given time. Cork these holes, fill the vessels with water, put in the corks with their rods, and set the taps running at the same time. Both rods will descend simultaneously to the line above which is written the message to be telegraphed. When a message is to be sent, the

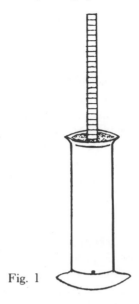

Fig. 1

sender first raises a fire signal to attract the observer's attention and waits until it is answered. Both will then set the taps running, and the sender will watch until the rod has descended to the line marking the message, when he will raise another fire signal. The receiver stops the water, and noting the mark on the rod at the edge of the vessel, will have the message. According to Polybius, this device is an improvement on the previous ones, but it still lacks range and detail, e.g. as to the enemy's number, where he has entered the country, etc. all of which are crucial to meeting the threat successfully.

Polybius later refers to another system invented by Cleonexus and Democlitus, about whom nothing is known, though they likely antedated Polybius (205?–125 B.C.) who claims to have perfected their system. But before turning to it, some summary observations are in order. First, from Homer, ca. the 8th cent. B.C., down to Polybius, the 2nd cent. B.C., no great advances seem to have been made in signalling at a distance. Except for the device of Aeneas, the simple fire signal or beacon light such as that described in Aeschylus'*Agamemnon*, seems to have been in general use. Second, it is in conjunction with Aeneas' system that writing is first mentioned by Polybius. Prior to that, the messages to be relayed were agreed on beforehand, or involved very simple signals with no knowledge of letters. Thucydides, for example, in his account of the Spartan attack on Salamis in 429 B.C. (2. 94) relates the use of fire signals to send messages from Salamis to Athens, and in his account the expression "hostile fire signals" (*phryktoi polemioi*) occurs. The Scholiast on the passage explains the expression as meaning that when the news of hostile movements was communicated, the signals (probably torches) were waved to and fro; when they referred to the approach of a friendly force, they were held steady. In any case, it still did not involve writing or a knowledge of letters, although it is often heralded as a significant development in the history of the ancient telegraph.[11]

Now the term "telegraph" literally means "writing at a distance," and the invention of Samuel B. Morse in the 19th century was a great advance in technology. For with the use of electric impulses, whole "written" messages could be conveyed from a distance, and in a short period of time. The success of the system obviously depends on a high degree of literacy, primarily the ability to convert dots and dashes into written messages. But in the Greek world, at least until Polybius' time, signalling at a distance did not depend on literacy but simply on messages orally agreed to before hand. One possible exception to this general observation, however, deserves mention, especially since it forms part of the evidence for literacy in Greek communities other than Athens where in the late 5th and 4th centuries B.C., literacy seems to have been widespread. The evidence comes from Sparta where there was a special method of sending dispatches to commanders on campaign. According to this method, a message was written on a strip of leather rolled slantwise, like a bandage, about a stick known as the *skytalē*. If the leather strip was removed from the stick, the message became unintelligible. But the Spartan commander to whom the leather strip was sent possessed an identical *skytalē*, of the same thickness, and by winding the strip around it, he could read the message. The device suggests, of course, that there was some literacy among the Spartans, but how much there is no way of knowing.[12] In any case, the *skytalē* is not technically an example of telegraphy or writing at a distance. As Diels noted, "this begins and ends with wireless telegraphy (*Funkentelegraphie*)," and since the ancient world did not have electricity at its technological disposal, this involved flashes from signal fires.[13]

It is now appropriate to return to Polybius, according to whom as system was perfected whereby words could be spelled out completely, using the great technological resource of the ancient world—fire. In its operation the system required more than normally close observation, and it is basically as follows. Divide the Greek alphabet into groups of five letters, in regular sequence, and write each group in order on a tablet of suitable height. Thus,

A	Z	Λ	Π	Φ
B	H	M	P	X
Γ	Θ	N	Σ	Ψ
Δ	I	Ξ	T	Ω
E	K	O	Y	

There are then five tablets, the last having only four letters. Each observer has a set of these tablets, and a stenoscope (*dioptron*) which limits, but does not magnify the field of vision. The stenoscope has two tubes enabling the observer

Fig. 2

to distinguish through one the right, through the other the left, position of the signal given opposite. To begin the communication, the sender raises two torches, the receiver responds with two to show that all is in order. To indicate the tablet to be observed, the sender raises one torch on the left for the first tablet, two for the second, and so forth. For the intended letter on the tablet, one torch on the right if for the first, two if for the second, three if for the third, etc. The message is to be reduced to the fewest possible letters. Suppose "Kretans" is to be sent: K is on the second tablet, fifth place; hence, raise two torches on the left, five on the right; R (or P, rho) fourth tablet, second place; hence, raise four torches on the left, two on the right, and so on.

The tablets are erected near the stenoscope, and a wall or screen is constructed on the right and on the left, for about ten feet high on each side, at the ends of which torches are raised so that the receiver can clearly distinguish the right position from the left, and the torches may be hidden when lowered behind the wall or screen. Polybius concludes with what can be considered a characteristic remark:

> for I have stated that in our time all arts and sciences have so much advanced
> that knowledge of most of them may be said to have been reduced to a system.
> This is, then, one of the most useful parts of history properly written.

So much is found in Polybius' account of the telegraph, but in discussing problems connected with its use, mainly the need for many torches, and much practice, Polybius uses an illustration which is of significance for the telegraph's connection with literacy:

> if we put side by side a man who is ignorant and unpracticed in letters, but
> generally intelligent, and a boy who is accustomed to read, give the boy a
> book and order him to read it, the man will plainly not be able to believe that
> a reader must first of all pay attention to the form of each letter, then to its
> sound-value, next to the combinations of the different letters. . . So when he
> sees that the boy without hesitation reels off five or seven lines in a breath he
> will not feel it easy to believe that he never read the book before, and he will
> absolutely refuse to believe this if the reader should be able to observe the ac-
> tion, the pauses, and the rough and smooth breathings.

Polybius' example illustrates, of course, the need for practice in using the telgraphic system described by him. Reading is the "clearest case of all" for the necessity of practice, and more generally, his example supports the need for not abandoning anything useful because of initial difficulty in learning it. Habit is necessary for learning, and through it, "all good things fall into the hands of men."

In his commentary on Polybius, Wallbank refers to the passage with the note that "for the adducing of reading as an analogy in argument cf. Plato. *Rep.* ii. 368D, iii. 402 A–B . . . Dion. Hal. *de comp. verb.* 25; *de Dem. vi in dicendo,* 52."[14] All relevant comparisons to be sure, but one wonders how common the lettered boy and illiterate man were in Polybius' time. Certainly the technicians involved in Polybius' telegraph, senders and receivers, need not necessarily have a high degree of literacy. Presumably with the tablets before them, they knew enough to transcribe the message, but were they capable of understanding it? The shortness of most messages suggests they were, but could they read and understand a long written passage? Moreover, how common were literate boys and unlettered men in Polybius' time? His use of an example that was uncommon would hardly seem a good illustration of his general point, and one can only infer that even in the 2nd cent. B.C. there were illiterate individuals incapable, say, of reading a passage of Homer or of Thucydides. It is, of course, difficult, if not impossible to gather statistics for literacy in various periods of the ancient world.[15] Indeed, the whole concept of literacy is not very clear—that there are or can be various levels of literacy is evident from any freshman English class. But certainly the development of the ancient telegraph from Homer onwards suggests a growing rise of literacy. The early beacon fires mentioned in Homer, Herodotus, Thucydides, did not depend on literacy—the telegraph of Polybius did to some extent since it involved at least a rudimentary knowledge of letters.

The close connection between the development of the ancient telegraph and the rise of literacy is further seen in the fact that only as there is an acoustical or optical means of relaying messages at a distance, can there be any meaningful use of the term "telegraph," literally "writing at a distance." Simple fire signals or beacon lights without reference to an alphabet or syllabary cannot easily be construed as a telegraph unless, of course, the latter term be extended to any kind of signal designed to convey a message. Certainly in modern, literate societies, the telegraph is closely linked with the alphabet and an ability to "read" messages (just as it was in Polybius' age). The modern telegraph is also connected with electricity (as it was not in Polybius' age), but this medium is not essential for a telegraph system. For, as Riepl observed, it is the alphabet which is primary:

> the alphabet (*Zeichenalphabet*) is primary for telegraphy whereas the means of relaying messages (*das Mittel der Übertragung*): electric current or blazing torch . . . electric sparks or wave-lengths . . . the brandished lance of a dragoon or of a Roman dictator . . . all that is secondary.[16]

In other words, it is the alphabet and literacy in general, not the means of conveying a written message, that is of importance in the concept of a telegraph. Thus, Cleonexus, Demokleitos, and Polybius grasped the basic notion of the telegraph, that is, conveying written messages at a distance, even though they may not have had the best means for doing this.

It is, of course, in connection with the practability of the Polybian system that problems arose. Since it was based on the reliability of human observation and vision, the great distances covered, as well as the complexity of translating messages into fire signals, obviously necessitated a large number of stations and signallers. Despite these factors, however, the Polybian system need not have been any more subject to error than the modern electrical telegraph. Yet it was precisely because of the need for vast human resources that the telegraph of Polybius probably proved impractical. To be sure, there was at least one attempt in antiquity to simplify the telegraph, and the evidence is found in the so-called *Kestoi* of Julius Africanus who probably lived in the 2nd cent. A.D. during the reigns of Elagabalus and Alexander Severus. But whether this system, like the Polybian, was actually used and by whom, remains unsure. In any case, it was a refinement on the Polybian system. The relevant Greek text is quoted by Riepl with his German translation.[17] In English it reads:

> Moreover, the Romans hit upon what is, in my opinion, an extremely amazing procedure in order to communicate with one another everything possible by means of fire signals. They limited the places provided for the use of fire signals, so that one is on the right, one is on the left, and one is in the middle. They then divided the letters among these three places, so that alpha to theta belongs in the place on the left, iota to pi in the middle place, and rho to omega in the place on the right. If they wanted, then, to signal "alpha," they raised once a fire signal on the left, for "beta" they raised a signal twice, for "gamma" three times and so forth. If they wanted to signal "iota," they raised a signal once in the middle, for "kappa" twice, and for "lamba" three times and so on. If they wanted to signal "rho," they raised a signal once on the right, two times for "sigma," and three times for "tau." They did this in order to avoid designating letters by means of a number of signals. For if they wanted to signal "rho," they did not raise an hundred fire signals, but as mentioned, raised only one signal on the right. They did this wholly in accord with those who received the signals; these copied letters indicated by means of the fire signals, read them, and signalled to those further on who were in charge of fire signals for the next station; these, then, in the same manner, relayed them to the following station until the message reached the last station.

According to Riepl, the Julian system was an advance over the Polybian "in dem grundsätzlichen Übergang von der Parallelität sur Sukzessivität der Zeichen," but without wholly eliminating the problems of Polybius' system.[18] For example, in contrast to the Polybian system, the number of places for fire signals was increased from two to three. At the same time, however, the tablets for the letters of the alphabet were reduced from five to three, and the number of signallers for a station was also reduced accordingly. In general, as Riepl correctly noted, the time it would take for a message to be relayed by the Polybian system was greatly reduced in the Julian, and "mit diesem, wie wir es nennen wollen, julianischen System verlohnte es sich unter Umständen tatsächlich zu telegraphieren." Whether, of course, the system was ever used, remains in doubt. [19]

The previous survey of the telegraph's development in the ancient world has yielded some interesting material for speculation, and the following remarks are for this purpose, and with no claim to finality. It has, of course, been seen that the telegraph provides some evidence for the rise and spread of literacy in the Greek and Roman worlds (the fire signals in Homer or in Aeschylus, for example, reveal no knowledge of letters). The extent, however, to which literacy spread and how quickly, are matters that will probably remain a subject of scholarly debate. Nonetheless, by the fourth century B.C. there seems to have been much more literacy than in previous centuries, and it is precisely in the fourth century that important technological innovations occur. One can only assume that literacy itself contributed, in part, to these, and that a technological society can only exist where there is a fair amount of literacy. For oral habits of mind emphasize memory and training, and a preoccupation with memory or memorized materials, together with more or less fixed traditions and established patterns of behavior, suggests an inability to deal with new and hitherto unexperienced situations. Given the flexibility and scope of the written word (as opposed to the almost formulaic, limited scope of the spoken) and its independence of memory, it is not surprising to find that the human mind is freed to deal with events and situations in a more innovative and complex manner. The telegraph itself represents some of the values of the literate mind, for by the use of written messages, it is able to signal not only what has happened, and in some detail, but also what is happening, or even may happen. In any case, the mind is no longer dependent on receiving previously (orally) agreed to messages, and it can entertain new and unexpected contingencies. Granted, of course, the telegraph could never become a really viable means of communication in the ancient world because of the lack of electricity; but it at least challenged the relatively "static" and fixed world of an oral culture. In connection with this last remark, it is interesting to note that the telegraph is given great theoretical (at least) attention at a time, beginning in the fourth century B.C., when the somewhat isolated world of Greece (isolated certainly since the Persian Wars), is once more being opened up to foreign influence with the conquests of Alexander and the creation of his far-flung "empire." That the telegraph should later be somewhat refined in the 2nd cent. A.D., is not surprising in view of the Romans' great need for holding a vast empire together.

That technological innovations, literacy aside, are often spawned by war, as certainly seems the case with the ancient telegraph, should come as no surprise, however distasteful the observation may be. The technological "block" of the ancient world, noted by Garlan, was often broken by external dangers. Again, the literate mind is perhaps better able to respond to these dangers and challenges from the outside than is the oral. To think of Harold Innis' views for a moment, there is much truth in his notion that ancient Rome had a spatial "bias" of communication which favored, among other things, easy transportability (e.g. papyri and imperial runners). In contrast to the durability or temporal bias of, say, ancient Babylon (e.g. with its not easily transportable clay tablets), Rome was more concerned with immediate, frequent, and often unpredictable situations, and hence with messages of limited duration.[20] Certainly the papyrus and telegraph favored these, and hence the conquest of space rather than time. Thus in the case of Rome and later Greece, the earlier, temporal bias of an oral culture, with its often small and localized institutions and its emphasis on durability, was offset by the spatial bias of a written language, and easy methods of transporting or relaying written messages.

Clearly, the ancient telegraph was before its time. It was based, to be sure, on writing, but it lacked electricity. In fact, the first major use of electronics in the nineteenth century was the modern telegraph. In any case, the ancient telegraph was an attempt to bridge the transition between an oral and literature culture, and no doubt other implications can be seen in its use. The fact remains that it shows the ancients struggling at their best with a then slowly changing world. They had the basic elements, the letters of an alphabet, but not the best way of working with these.

NOTES AND REFERENCES

[1] Especially useful for details on the ancient telegraph and its development are: H. Diels, *Antike Technik*, 3rd ed. (Leipzig-Berlin 1924) esp. 71–90 which are devoted to "antike Telegraphie"; A.C. Merriam, "Telegraphing Among the Ancients," *Papers of the Archaeological Institute of America*, Class. Series 3, no. 1 (1890) 1–32; and W. Riepl, *Das Nachrichtenwesen des Altertums* (Leipzig-Berlin 1913) esp. 46–122. Riepl provides the fullest and most detailed account, and any study of the ancient telegraph should probably begin with his.

[2] All translations of Polybius are those of W. R. Paton, *Polybius: the Histories*, IV of Loeb Classical Library (Cambridge, Mass., reprint 1968).

[3] On Aeneas, see F. W. Wallbank, A *Historical Commentary on Polybius* II (Oxford 1967) 259, and E. Schwartz, "Aeneias (3)," in *Paulys Real-Encyclopädie der classischen Altertumswissenschaft* I (Stuttgart 1894) cols. 1019–21.

[4] These references are taken from Merriam's "Telegraphing"; others are found in Diels, *Antike*, and Riepl, *Nachrichtenwesen*. The translation of *Ag.* 9–10 is that of R. Lattimore, *Aeschylus: Oresteia* (Chicago, reprint 1967).

5 For the inventions of Palamedes, and the various stories associated with him, see E. Wüst, "Palamedes (1)," in *Paulys Real-Encyclopädie der classischen Altertumswissenschaft* XVIII (Stuttgart 1942) cols. 2500–2512.

6 Riepl, *Nachrichtenwesen*, 75. Riepl writes:

> Während im Osten die Feuersignale zwar auch vornehmlich eigentlichen militärischen, strategischen und taktischen Zwecken, aber daneben auch ebenso dem nichtmilitärischen Nachrichtenverkehr dienstbar gemacht werden, besonders der Fernübertragung politischer Nachrichten, und in den vorhistorischen Zeiten die nichtmilitärischen Signale sogar überwiegen, *findet sich in der ganzen römischen Geschichte nur ein einziges Beispiel von einem eigentlichen Nachrichtensignal, nämlich die Depesche vom Sturze Sejans, welche sich Tiberius von Rom nach Capri durch Signale übermitteln lässt.*

The italics are mine.

7 Suetonius. *Tiberius* 65. The translation is that of R. Graves, *Suetonius: The Twelve Caesars* (Harmondsworth, reprint 1970).

8 Diels, *Antike*, 90.

9 See H. W. Pleket, "Technology and Society in the Graeco-Roman World," *Acta Historiae Neerlandica* 2 (Leiden 1967) 1–25, esp. 6–10.

10 Y. Garlan, *War in the Ancient World: A Social History* (New York 1975) 185.

11 See Riepl, *Nachrichtenwesen*, 59–60.

12 On the *skytalē* and the assessment of literacy in the ancient world, see David Harvey, "Literacy in the Athenian Democracy," *REG* 74 (1966) 585–635, esp. 625–627 for the *skytalē*.

13 Diels, *Antike*, 76. Diels' remark follows his discussion of messenger pigeons ("die Taubenpost"); he also discusses the *skytalē* on 72–73 and the "Depeschenrad" mentioned in Aeneas Tacitus.

14 Wallbank, *Commentary on Polybius*, 261.

15 See, for example, R. MacMullen, *Roman Government's Response to Crises, A.D. 235–337* (New Haven 1976) 201. MacMullen writes:

> After 250 statistical services probably deteriorated all over the empire, manifestly so in Egypt. The average citizen's literacy and numeracy continued their own steady decline, too.

16 Riepl, *Nachrichtenwesen*, 94.

17 *Ibid.*, 107–08.

18 *Ibid.*

19 *Ibid.*, 109.

20 See H. A. Innis' works, specially, *Empire and Communications* (London 1950) and *The Bias of Communication* (Toronto 1951).

Born in Canada Professor CHRISTINE MITCHELL HAVELOCK was educated at the University of Toronto and Harvard. In 1951 she was obliged to refuse a Fulbright Fellowship in order to accept the Charles Eliot Norton Fellowship at the American School of Classical Studies in Athens.

Upon arrival in Athens, she almost immediately found the subject of her dissertation when she spied the reliefs on a triangular base in the Agora Museum. It was just after the civil war and some sections of the city were barricaded, and when the young student traveled down the Peloponnese to a remote temple at Bassae she rode a donkey.

Returning to Harvard where she acquired her doctorate, the Phi Beta Kappa scholar taught at Harvard and Wellesley and in 1953 joined the Vassar faculty, where she now holds the Sarah Gibson Blanding Chair in Liberal Arts and Sciences. More recently she became an Associate Fellow of Timothy Dwight College in Yale University.

In the intervening years, in addition to numerous articles and reviews, she has written a distinguished book, *Hellenistic Art: The Art of the Classical World from the Death of Alexander to the Battle of Actium* which views Hellenistic art as an enrichment rather than a decline of classical styles. Published in 1971 by the New York Graphic Society and the Phaidon Press in London, it has since appeared in German and Polish editions.

Professor Havelock's students call her *dame de noblesse*. A recent Vassar publication describes her as "an example of the strong, exceptional, independent woman on which Vassar's international reputation has always rested."

Art as Communication in Ancient Greece

by *CHRISTINE M. HAVELOCK*

How did the ancient Greek react to the art which surrounded him? What sort of impact did temples, statues and paintings have upon him? What did the planners and makers of these works of art hope to achieve? What did they want to communicate?

These questions are not often asked, and they are not easy to answer.[1] To begin with, the word "art" as we tend to understand it was not used by the classical Greeks. *Technē* which has been translated as "rational production" was the term they most commonly used in referring to art. It does not imply a separate and superior endeavor undertaken by geniuses.[2] However, the questions which are posed here may be at least partially answered. Ancient literary and epigraphical sources cast some light on the purpose and effect of art. While these documents are frequently impersonal, they sometimes betray the writer's feelings and preferences. What we can be sure of is that, in antiquity, Greek art did not communicate in the learned language we currently use to interpret a statue or relief. Since the evidence seems to indicate that most Greeks of the archaic and early classical periods were at best semi-literate[3], messages therefore contained in the visual arts must have been composed for maximum effect, and the impression they made must have been particularly vivid and immediate. This paper will attempt to intercept a few of these visual messages, chronologically remote though they may be, and to reconstruct, in some measure, the ancient experience of a work of art.

PART I

No author of pagan antiquity has provided us with anything like as illuminating a document as the contemporary account by Procopius of the building of Hagia Sophia in Constantinople (532–537 A.D.). Procopius, an historian, was quite explicit as to the way the architecture and mosaics visually and spiritually affected the Christian beholder. Indeed, he writes from the point of view of the spectator. He was himself present during the construction of the church; he describes plan and elevation and he declares on the basis of his experience that the designers have outwitted the observer by obscuring structural logic. The dome . . . "seems not to rest on solid construction but to hang by a golden cord from heaven to cover space . . . The beholders cannot let their sight rest fondly on any one point, for each attracts the eye and makes it travel easily to itself . . . and thus those who have studied every part, and bent their brows over them all, fail to understand the art, but go away struck by what to the sight is incomprehensible." Therefore, "when one goes there to pray he straightway understands that it is not by human power or art but by the influence of God that this work is fashioned."[4] Justinian, Procopius tells us, supervised the details of the building, visited it during construction, and when it was completed proclaimed that it surpassed in beauty the temple of Solomon. One could argue that no art historian has yet surpassed Procopius' description of the transcendental effects of this building and the manner in which they were achieved.

Much earlier, in classical Greece, an equal amount of labor, expense, and thought went into the building and decoration of the Parthenon. Judging by the unity and uniqueness of the architectural and sculptural design, we may surmise that Pericles took as keen an interest in the project as Justinian did in Hagia Sophia. Yet the longest ancient description we have of the Parthenon, which at the time of its origin and still today stands as the epitome of Greek ideas and aspirations, is dry, disappointing and incomplete. It was written by Pausanias (c.170 A.D.) more than 500 years after its erection. He personally visited the temple, which was still in perfectly good condition, and here is the sort of thing he says about it: "All the figures in the gable over the entrance to the temple called the Parthenon relate to the birth of Athena. The back gable contains the strife of Poseidon with Athena for the possession of the land. The image itself is made of ivory and gold . . . The image of Athena stands upright, clad in a garment that reaches to her feet: on her breast is the head of Medusa wrought in ivory. In one hand she holds a Victory about four cubits high, and in the other a spear. . . ." (*Description of Greece*, I, 24, 5–7). Pausanias remained utterly unmoved. He says nothing about the impact of this magnificent temple on himself or on anyone else.

Plutarch (c.100 A.D.) is certainly less stilted. I refer to his account of the Periclean building program which he enthusiastically praises for its "shining grandeur . . . beauty and freshness . . ." As a consequence, he says, the buildings will make a favorable impression and convince everyone of the power and wealth of Athens. This was true, but compared to Procopius' sophisticated appraisal of Hagia Sophia, how little we learn about the Parthenon. Plutarch's praise is conventional; he never singles out the temple as the jewel of the program. He does not even describe it. He is much more concerned to show that Pericles was justified in starting the whole enterprise as an economic boon to the city and people of Athens (*Life of Pericles*, 12–13).

The only contemporary documentation concerning the Parthenon which has come down to us is the building inscriptions.[5] While they are of economic interest, they hardly contribute to our aesthetic understanding. In short, in antiquity no one wrote at length of the Parthenon as an architectural marvel the way Procopius wrote of Hagia Sophia.

Unfortunately the majority of ancient writers are not systematically informative about the artistic purpose or effect of any Greek art monument. Yet, directly or indirectly, we can learn what the Greeks liked and what impressed them. Therefore, we will briefly survey a number of writings which in one way or another reveal the response of the observer. We will be less interested in professional theories, criticism, or literary parallels. We want to try to see and react as the ancient Greeks saw and reacted. We may begin by examining the factors in a work of art which appealed to them.

Intrinsic value and brilliance of the material

The Greek eye liked to be dazzled. Anything that was made of a precious material was highly prized especially if it sparkled. Color and brightness in themselves gave pleasure. This is, of course, a universal preference but it seems to have been particularly strong among the Greeks. Homer (c.750 B.C.) spoke frequently of "gleaming bronze armor" and "glittering gold nails." "Take a look, son of Nestor . . . at the gleam of bronze in the echoing halls, and of gold and amber, of silver and ivory; the court of Zeus the Olympian must be like this inside." (*Odyssey*, 4, 71) Homer does not react in the same degree to the colors of nature. It is also evident that gold, silver, bronze, ivory, amber and precious stones—whether in jewelry, armor or houses—denoted the owner's status and wealth, and for this reason, too, were admired. Herodotus, the historian, (c.450 B.C.) was not much interested in art objects as such, yet he was fascinated by the Lydian kings' fabulous gifts made of precious metals to Apollo at Delphi. Again these are status symbols. Their weight and value are furnished and the repetitive intoning of the words "gold" and "silver" serves to bring this shimmering mass of objects into imaginative reality (*History*, 1, 50–52, 92). Classical tragic and comic poets heighten their dramatic effects by studding their lines, where appropriate, with references to gold and silver objects or decoration. "She undid her robe, where the brooch of beaten gold was set upon her breast" and then Deianeira plunges the sword into her side (Sophocles, *The Women of Trachis*, 924–930).

The sun-like radiance of gold and the polish of silver (as well as their cost) made these metals appropriate for cult statues, royal gifts or for ceremonies in which pomp and circumstance were expected, such as the funeral procession of Alexander the Great (Diodorus Siculus, *World History*, 18, 26, 3ff). But they could assist the erotic as well as the political occasion. Jewelry of precious metals worn by women enhanced their value as love objects and hence their powers of seduction. When Hera prepares herself to seduce Zeus in Book 14 of the *Iliad* she makes sure she "shines" all over—and gold and silver ornaments and clothing produced the desired result. Likewise in Apollonius' *Argonautica* (3rd century B.C.), Medea lays a silver veil over "golden tresses" before she receives Jason with whom she has just fallen in love. Later they proceed to a bridal couch covered with the golden fleece (3, 828–833; 4, 1141–1143).

Craftsmanship

Living as we do in an industrial age, we are sometimes indifferent to the quality of work which goes into the making of an art object. To the Greeks the performance of a craft was a very important occupation which had its divine patrons, Athena and Hephaistos. An artist was first and foremost a craftsman, and to qualify as such, a work of art had to be skillfully made. "Well-wrought" was a frequent epithet for a hand-made object; it evoked even stronger praise if it was ornate and elaborate. A Greek artist had to be a hard worker to be great. The bronze shield of the hero Achilles is Homer's literary invention. But as an ideal shield it called for a vast design laden with decoration and narrative incident (*Il.*, 18, 468ff). To honor Apollo properly, his archaic throne at Amyclae, made by Bathycles, contained a prodigious quantity of figurative reliefs which are described in full by Pausanias (*Description*, 3, 18). In pursuit of their philosophical objectives both Plato and Aristotle linger on the idea of art as technique and on the obligations of the craftsman toward his work. Aristotle, who made the more definitive statement, stressed that the artist must have a knowledge of the material with which he works and that he must use his brains to manipulate the material toward the desired end.[6] The comic poet Hipparchus (c. 260 B.C.) wrote a play about a painter, in the course of which these memorable words are uttered: "Of all possessions, the one that is in the eyes of all men by far the most valued in life is technical skill. For all things else war and the vicissitudes of fortune bring to ruin, but technique is saved."[7] Lysippos is Pliny the Elder's favorite sculptor, and one of the reasons was undoubtedly that he carved more statues than anyone else (*Natural History*, 34, 61). In another passage, Pliny thinks it important to tell us that the large sculptured groups of the Laocoon and the "Farnese Bull" were each carved out of one piece of stone (*N.H.*, 31, 33–37). His report may have been erroneous, but we learn from it what kind of artistic achievement Pliny considered remarkable.[8]

Good building techniques were also appreciated: Odysseus visits the palace of Alkinoos and before he steps over the threshold he takes in the sturdy walls, the elegant fittings and the ingenious decorations (*Od.*, 7, 81ff). Occasionally Pausanias can be impressed by stone work (Tiryns, Propylaea, and finally, Vitruvius in his treatise *De Architectura* (late first century B.C.), the only one of its kind to survive from antiquity, asserts, in line with Aristotle, that the "proper management of materials" is one of the nine fundamental principles upon which good architecture depends (Book I, chapter 2).

Lifelikeness, story, action

The Greeks instinctively responded to and appreciated lifelikeness in a work of art. "Lifelikeness" should here be interpreted in a broad but literal sense, as "having similarity to life" or "seeming to be alive." It may or may not also mean realistic representation or the faithful replica of a model.

In the archaic and classical periods a clear distinction between the made object and the reality is frequently absent. That is, the sculpture may be thought to be physically comprised of flesh and blood. Thus, a statue can sometimes reach out, as it were, and address the spectator: "Mantiklos . . . dedicated me to the Far-Darter," says a little bronze warrior from Thebes now in the Boston Museum of Fine Arts.[9] The message is inscribed on his thighs. The statuette, in early Orientalizing style, is anything but realistic and yet it is vividly alive and can speak. Even a non-human object can, in the archaic period, take on a life of its own—as when an inscription on a pot reads "I greet you."[10]

The chorus in Euripides' *Ion*, a drama which takes place in the sanctuary at Delphi, breaks into song when it looks around at the sculpture which possibly decorated the pediment of the Temple of Apollo. It is hard to believe they sing about stone figures. "Look where the Lernaean monster falls! See how the son of Zeus can ply his golden scimitar! . . . I see! And there's another close beside who lifts a sparkling torch . . . And do you see—there, brandishing her gorgon shield against her enemy—It's Pallas (Athena)! the goddess of my city and my own!".[11] With popping eyes, the chorus exclaims about what they see, not as if they were objective works of art, but as if instead Herakles, Iolaos or Athena were right there in front of them fully alive and in action. There exists here, and in the earlier examples, an easy communication between statuary and the observer, as if they were similar beings, with an implied two-way participation. One is consequently tempted to think, that in an effort to strengthen this participation and mutual identification, the sculptures were fashioned more and more to outwardly resemble their human counterparts. Does this help to explain the evolution of Greek art and the realistic qualities found in later sculpture?[12]

At other times, the distinction between the stone statue and the real person or model is underlined and, at the same time, the similarity is remarked upon. The inherent contradiction or contrast can lead to dramatic and also amusing situations. Admetus, in Euripides' *Alcestis*, considers consoling himself for the death of his wife in this manner: "And by an artist's handicraft thy form/ shall be/ fashioned resting at length upon a couch;/ and I shall/ fall upon it and clasp it in my arms/ and call thy name and fancy that I have/ my dear wife in my embrace, *though I have her not.*"[13]

The ironic difference between appearance and reality increases in the Hellenistic period. In the first half of the third century there is a charming conversation between two gossipy women in Herodas' fourth *Mime*. They are walking in the sanctuary of Asklepios at Cos and, seeing the statuary, they squeal with delight: "Oh my . . . what beautiful statues . . . Look dearie, look at that child gazing upward toward the apple. Wouldn't you say that if she doesn't get that apple she might expire on the spot? And look at that old man . . . and look how that child strangles the Egyptian goose. If the stone weren't in front of us, this, you might say, would start talking. My, my! The time will come when man will put real life into these stones!"[14] The two women are deeply affected and impressed by the immediacy and the life of the figures. Also, it seems to me that Herodas is especially perspicacious in choosing the kind of subject-matter with which, as women, they could most easily identify and might even try to confuse with reality.

Pliny remains in this tradition when, through anecdote, he suggests there is no barrier between the observer and the work of art. We can learn from him also how powerful art can be and how helpless and controllable the spectator is when confronted by it. Pliny's anecdotes seem fantastic and his observer's reactions naive, yet they are universal and persistent reactions. Lifelike (not necessarily realistic)[15] representation appears to be the clue. The painted or sculptured object is mistaken for the real thing and the spectator responds in a predictable fashion. Thus, birds peck at painted grapes and horses neigh when they see their painted peers (N.H. 35, 65, 95). Or, sexual appetites are aroused at the sight of nudity or physical beauty, as when one man loses his self-control while gazing at the Aphrodite of Knidos (N.H. 36, 20). *Idyll* 15 of Theocritus

(3rd century) describes how a statue of Adonis sends terrific shivers through the girls from Syracuse attending a festival at Alexandria. There is also the perennial Greek story of the man from Samos who fell in love with a marble maiden and locked himself up in the temple. Pygmalion was the victim of the same illusion. Lucian will tell you all about a painting he has himself seen—the wedding of Alexander and Roxane. The description does not read like a verbal duplicate of a framed two dimensional illusion, but as a romantic spectacle or stage play filled with erotic incident: "There is a very beautiful chamber and a marriage bed, and on it Roxane is seated, represented as a virgin of great beauty, whose eyes are cast down toward the ground in modesty, since Alexander stands nearby. There are also some smiling Cupids. One of them, standing behind her, draws the veil from her head and shows Roxane to the bridegroom; another, in the manner of a true servant, is taking the sandal from her foot as if he were already preparing her for bed; still another figure, this one also being a Cupid, has taken hold of Alexander's mantle, and is pulling him toward Roxane, using all his strength to drag him." [16]

"Lifelikeness," defined in this paper as "seeming to be alive," contains another important factor—to be alive presumes movement or the ability to move. The Greeks liked to see action, but meaningful action involving a story or myth. They loved a good tale and they could easily recognize what was going on; they did not rely on labels. [17] This recognition itself caused pleasure, as Aristotle reluctantly acknowledged in the *Poetics*. The pleasure the chorus of the *Ion* feels is partly derived from the liveliness of the action—falling, playing, brandishing, etc., but there is additional enjoyment in the speed with which they identify the hydra, Herakles, and Athena in turn. The Greeks had their myths committed to memory and it did not take much by way of a visual sign to remind them of the full story. [18]

Consistent with the preoccupation with story and action is the emphasis on the human figure and, to a lesser extent, animals. The chorus in the *Ion* remains impervious to the spectacular scenery in which the sanctuary of Apollo is situated. It is not nature that enraptures them, but men or man-like gods in action. Pausanias is again a case in point. His *Description of Greece* constitutes a kind of Baedeker to the ancient sites and cities. He visited personally building after building, and yet he is extremely reticent about architecture as such. He will abbreviate the description of a major temple, such as the Parthenon, or the temple of Zeus at Olympia, and then proceed, it seems with haste, to a lengthy documentation of the figurative ornamentation, its authorship and subject-matter. He will identify individual people, represented in statuary, by name; his list of athletic victors at Olympia is astonishingly long. He appears to look right at each one, and the sport itself, the activity, is always mentioned as a part of the identification (*Description of Greece*, IV, 1–16).

Pliny was not writing a guidebook, so he had more reason to curtail his observations on architecture, but he too betrays a bias in favor of sculpture and painting. For instance, to him, the Mausoleum of Halicarnassos was one of the

Seven Wonders, not because of its size or unusual pyramidal crown, but because the sculptors Scopas, Timotheos, Leochares and Bryaxis had devotedly worked on it (*N.H.* 36, 30–31). In his treatise on architecture, Vitruvius repeatedly finds it necessary to interject the human figure—he argues that the proportions of the Doric and Ionic Orders were copied as a matter of course from the proportions of the body of a man and woman respectively. The validity of this theory does not concern us, but it does suggest that the architect Vitruvius instinctively assumed that architectural rules could be justified only if they were derived from the human body, that is, from life (*De Architectura*, Bk. 3, Ch. 1 Bk. 5, Ch. 1).

So far, literary sources have revealed that, in regard to works of art, the ancient observer was impressed and delighted by precious materials, expert craftsmanship and a good story contained in lifelike action. In a sense, we could say that all these qualities aroused feelings of pleasure and enjoyment. Yet two major ancient writers, Plato and Aristotle, realized that art communicated, perhaps subliminally, more than pleasure, and that it was therefore a very serious matter. Since they both wrote in the fourth century B.C., long before Pliny, Pausanias or Vitruvius, they surely have a better understanding of art and its function and place in classical times. Their views are of the greatest importance in answering the questions set by this paper. They are especially important because they are not altogether at variance with, but instead confirm, those already cited from later writers. Both Plato and Aristotle were concerned with the notion of lifelikeness in the arts. But instead of expressing approval of it, they were deeply disturbed.

As is well known, Plato's main worry was the harmful impact poetry might have on the ordinary person. He assumed, chiefly in the *Republic*, that a lifelike action, described in narrative form as in epic or rendered in dramatic poetic form on the stage, would stimulate a real-life action of an identical kind in the listener or observer. He thought people automatically imitated what they heard and saw. This made painting suspect, too. He was bothered, for instance, by the couch which the artist paints because he thought the observer would mistake it for a real one made by a carpenter. The point is that this indicates the degree to which Plato also believed the painted world and the real world could become confused or meshed in the eye and mind of the naive spectator. Any successful painter, he rather scornfully argued, would prefer to get out and *do* the heroic deeds he rendered on a two-dimensional surface. This may seem ridiculous to us, but such a thought on Plato's part again indicates how strongly he thought men would identify with and be motivated by the action in a work of art. Since he did not approve of the poetry then current he felt obliged to banish it from his ideal state. By implication, painting must go, too. But, we wonder, was not sculpture much more dangerous? Sculptures are three-dimensional rather than two-dimensional representations; are they not, then, closer to reality or nature even than painting? Plato did not enter such a debate. He does, however, make a concession which is important to the art historian. Works of art may be morally acceptable if they are designed in a certain way: "For disorder and lack of pattern and unfittingness are the kin of evil speech and evil character, but their opposites, on the contrary, are kin and imitations of moderation and noble character." (*Republic*, 401A). According to Plato, only geometry can make art respectable.

Plato's fears about art should be understood in the context of mimesis, or imitation, which permeates much thinking in antiquity.[19] To sum up, according to him the observer should be exposed to worthy examples of behaviour in dramatic poetry and in the visual arts, so that he can imitate or model himself after them. Surely this reflects Plato's understanding of the purpose and inevitable effect of works of art.

The moral ingredient is also embedded in Aristotle's views on art. Like Plato, he was primarily interested in poetry, with painting only introduced by way of analogy. To Aristotle, some painters are superior to others because they inspire good rather than bad behaviour, for the simple reason that they paint people with good rather than bad character. The nature of their character, we should note, can be known because it is represented through their actions. If art will furnish models proper for people to imitate, let us have it, he argues. Thus both Plato and Aristotle were aware that art had a psychological effect because it constantly relayed moral or immoral messages, not just optical pleasures, to the spectator.[20]

Our next task is to try to detect some of these visual signals from the works of art themselves. The messages were communicated to the ancient Greek observer officially and unofficially, publicly and privately, by the architecture he saw and used, by the sculpture which decorated it or stood nearby, and by the paintings on the cups he drank from at home or at parties.

PART II: OFFICIAL ART

The most significant type of building in ancient Greece was the temple (fig. 1). Time and thought, money and labor were lavished upon its construction and decoration. Temples were public, not private. There were a good many of them scattered in town or *temenos*. As state or civic institutions, they embodied the religious and political ideas of the Greek people. They were normally conspicuous and well-situated, frequently the largest building of a city or sanctuary. Thus, their importance was made clear through sheer visibility. Moreover, a Greek temple had an enduring and characteristic form. Therefore, while he seldom may have entered it, it was a structure which any Greek would have immediately recognized. Given the slower pace of life, he would subsequently have had both the time and inclination to absorb some of its subtleties which were calculated to engage his interest and arouse his pleasure. Since the subtleties were so longlasting and pervasive, they must surely have done so.

At all periods, an unusual sensitivity to certain visual effects and details is

Fig. 1.   Parthenon, Athens, (photo Alison Frantz)

evident in Greek temple design. Because it was external, large and repeated, the column was the most striking element of the temple. It is a simple shape, it is clear, and to the Greeks, who saw it just about everywhere, it must have been familiar and therefore initially reassuring. Its roundness and tapering profile imbue it with life and movement or, in our definition, with lifelikeness. But every part of the temple had something to say to the observer, and something to do. The Greek eye was expected to understand structural logic and interrelationships. How else are we to explain the details of the Doric Order: the careful placing of the triglyph about the column, the entasis and fluting of the shaft, and horizontal curvature? Platform, peristyle and pediment are rationally related and their structural interdependence is deliberately made evident. The Ionic Order is also a logical system of standardized parts. In both orders, the interrelationships and subtleties are aesthetically pleasing. But their functional clarity, especially of the column, also encouraged the mind and, sympathetically the body, to respond actively. In short the Greek temple is the original architecture of humanism.[21] In general form and details it signaled to the observer, first, that he should seek order and stability and, secondly, that with effort, it was possible to achieve them. This is an optimistic visual message. The modern bank, with its Greek columns, still sends the same signal.

Yet there was more to communicate. Many Greek temples received decoration in the form of sculpture in the pediment, in the metopes, or along the frieze. As a rule, human or semihuman figures, rather than abstract or floral ornament, occupied these areas. The attention of the observer would thus be easily elicited as he approached the temple. He would find himself automatically, yet probably unconsciously, identifying with the sculptured figures, especially those of the pediment as the largest crowning feature. The identification would probably be more intense in the fifth than in the sixth century. As we know from such examples as the Temple of Artemis at Corfu, or the several limestone compositions from the Acropolis in Athens, the early archaic age tended to favor fantastic monsters rather than human beings in prominent positions in the pediment.[22]

We suppose also that the subject matter of the pedimental sculpture was recognized almost involuntarily by the spectator. There are several reasons for this, some of which are formal. Located at some distance from the observer, clarity in every sense was considered essential. Because of the triangular shape of the gable, the sculptured decoration was, with the usual Greek logic, centrally focussed (Fig. 2). The observer's eye, consequently, would be spared confusion. In respect to meaning, psychological nuances or complicated personal relationships were thought undesirable; simple physical actions in "intelligible poses" would convey the story or message most strongly and quickly.[23] This is precisely what we find in Greek pedimental decoration: one or more, but always a restricted number of events which are manifested entirely as physical actions. Nor would the actions be difficult to interpret; they would comprise a mythological event. The Greek observer would simply assume this; it was the custom and he had no reason to expect surprises or startling innovations. Indeed sculptured themes on Greek temples—whether in pediment, metope, or frieze—are noticeably repetitive and restricted.[24] The ancient worshipper,

Fig. 2   Battle of Lapiths and Centaurs, West Pediment, Temple of Zeus, Olympia (reconstruction)

who probably did not read easily, if at all, but who would have memorized his myths by heart, could be expected, as Aristotle well knew, to identify the theme of a pediment. The chorus did so in the *Ion*. Moreover, he might have seen the composition in some other context which would have made it still easier to recognize.[25] The myth might have panhellenic significance and the observer would surely know it. It could, on the other hand, have special local pertinence or possibly relevance to the deity to whom the temple was dedicated. The Greek spectator was an easy and knowledgeable target for visual messages, if not for propaganda.

It is difficult to think of a Greek temple which, if decorated, did not contain a battle scene somewhere.[26] Four in particular were repeatedly portrayed: the two great struggles of Greeks against the Centaurs and the Amazons, the Gods versus the Giants, and the Trojan War.[27] To a Greek, "war was a way of life," an aspect of the human condition and therefore inescapable.[28] Of this he was constantly reminded by the art around him. These graphic battles were not entirely remote nor necessarily divorced from the present; the classical Greek did not have our sense of history or concept of time. The past flowed into the present: Trojans could be Persians, giants could be Gauls; a battle between his fellow Greeks and a tribe of centaurs at a wedding could seem like a recent occurrence. Furthermore, a battle was, in a sense, fun; the observer could get right in there, so to speak, and take part empathetically. He is encouraged to do this because a one-to-one confrontation is, throughout Greek art, the norm. Consequently, the spectator would find himself personally involved in the action. He would instinctively, but imaginatively, enter into participation. In other words, his martial tendencies were encouraged and he was urged to fight as a hero.

Still another message would reach him: victory over one's opponents is never easy or guaranteed. The outcome of these battles in temple sculpture is often in doubt—as if it were unimportant. The Centauromachy on the west pediment of the temple of Zeus at Olympia is a case in point (Fig. 2): if we exclude the women, the protagonists are equal in number and neither one is winning. In the west pediment of the Parthenon, Poseidon and Athena are shown as completely equal competitors, each equipped with chariot and supported by allies.[29] Athena thus does not appear even here, in her own major temple, as the victor, even though the spectator would be aware that she actually was. In short, these scenes are not significant as triumphs of good over evil forces such as one might find in a Romanesque portal.

What aroused the greatest pleasure and enjoyment in the spectator however—if we are to judge by the frequency of representations—were the battles of the moral hero, Herakles. In Greek art, he is almost the perpetual "Man of the Year," being featured abundantly in sculpture and painting, as well as in poetry, in mainland Greece, in Asia Minor and in the Greek west. So often Herakles is an energetic actor taking on some adversary, man or beast, in direct combat. Rarely is he shown completely triumphant; he is usually in the midst

Fig. 3   Herakles bringing the Stymphalian birds to Athena, metope, Temple of Zeus, Olympia

of battle. If his labor has concluded, he is far from arrogant (Fig. 3). His opponents are always worthy and they are usually not just a problem to Herakles but also to mankind in general. By pitting himself against them, Herakles not only tests his own strength but also performs a wider humanitarian service. Consider, then, the multiple messages being sent to Greek youths to fight bravely and dauntlessly. They must have idolized Herakles; he was a real achiever, highly competitive, and eventually rewarded with immortality. He was also an intrepid explorer; his exploits occur in different geographical areas and all Greek youths, no matter where they lived, could be expected to find some psychological link with him. What better role model could there be?

Although battle scenes predominate in Greek architectural sculpture, the exceptions are perhaps even more interesting. Combats depict the world in strife, but the other side of the coin, the world in harmony, was also frequently represented. In the archaic Temple of Apollo at Delphi a battle between the gods and the giants occupied the west pediment. In the pediment of the main facade, the god himself appeared in his chariot accompanied by other members of the divine family and his good friends the Muses.[30] With this epiphany—a calm and dignified one—the spectator would, I think, be assured that everything was all right and in its proper place, and that while struggle was man's lot, its resolution was possible. Indeed, it became almost a classical formula to combine in one temple conflict and concord. On the temple of Zeus at Olympia, Pelops and Oinamaos prepare for their chariot race in the east pediment (Fig. 4). The scene is remarkably serene and orderly. There is no tension and there is no sense of foreboding or doom visible in composition, pose or facial expression.[31] All of this is in contrast to the west pediment which features an agile Centauromachy.

There is more flurry and excitement as Athena is born in the east pediment of the Parthenon, yet again nothing is out of control. The cosmos is a friendly one, a regular and rhythmic system guaranteed, it is inferred, by Athena's birth. However, the pediment transmits this heartening message primarily by means of the geometric arrangement of the sculpture.[32]

But on the Parthenon, no decoration would catch the attention and appreciation of the classical spectator more vividly than the cella frieze which depicts the Panathenaic procession (Fig. 5). Here past and present overlap, various categories of Athenian citizens are included, and therefore nearly all can psychologically participate.[33] If Pericles intended to elicit loyalty, pride and conforming behavior from his Athenians, the subject of the frieze and its style, which again consists of a conspicuously ordered composition, were exactly the right vehicle. Here we might remind ourselves that Plato felt that "disordered" art was morally reprehensible and deserved to be eradicated. It would be difficult to maintain that the sculpture of the Parthenon, indeed that of any Greek building, did not come up to his standard.[34]

Fig. 4   Preparation for a Chariot Race, East Pediment, Temple of Zeus, Olympia (reconstruction)

Fig. 5   Section of frieze, Parthenon, Paris, Louvre

It has been frequently said that an ancient Greek site must have appeared unbearably encumbered and cluttered. Sanctuaries, market places, cemeteries and roadsides, even house entrances, were usually decorated with statuary, dedications, or votives. Thus the spectator not only had architectural sculpture to enjoy, he also had nearly perpetual contact with statues or reliefs of gods, heroes, athletes and warriors (Fig. 6). The round sculptures were often very close to life-size and stood on relatively low pedestals. From this we can deduce that they were intended to have a reality and an existence comparable to the spectator's. There is no other way, it seems to me, to understand their materiality, their lifelike qualities (painted lips, eyeball, hair, drapery edges, etc.), and potential movement. When the spectator also observed that men and gods looked very much the same, a feeling of well-being and self-confidence ensued. He might also conclude it was within his capacity to imitate such athletes and warriors. The facial features of the statues were generalized enough to permit anyone to aspire to be like them. When Greek society honored its gods and heroes by erecting lifelike statues, it laid a claim on the emotional loyalties and behavior of the observer. Plato and Aristotle were certainly right in their judgment about the importance of the impact of art.

Today, we are aware that society transmits signals to the two sexes which affect their self-estimate and the roles each can expect to play. Ancient Greece had a wide assortment of such signals, verbal as well as visual. In the public arena, the visual signs suggested that heroic behaviour was primarily male. In this respect, Herakles is of supreme importance as a role model—for men. His prominence in painting and sculpture is a sure indication of the masculine ori-

Fig. 6   Bronze Ballplayer, National Museum, Athens

entation of the Greek world. When women behaved with the independence and bravery of men, they were regarded as enemies and as unnatural. That this possibility frequently occurred to the Greeks we can judge from the prevalence of Amazonomachies.[35] While other females are by no means excluded from monumental Greek art they appear, by and large, as helpers or assistants: Herakles and Theseus perpetually depend on Athena's support (Fig. 3), Oinomaos and Pelops must have their women with them before the chariot race (Fig. 4), Apollo needs the Muses to back him up, and a few young girls, reduced to a very small minority, offer their services in the Panathenaic procession (Fig. 5). In a story depicted on the inner frieze of the Altar of Zeus in Pergamon of Hellenistic date, Telephos' mother sees that he eventually establishes a dynasty.[36]

However, one woman, the goddess Athena, was celebrated in the visual arts to an unusual degree all over the Greek world as well as in Athens. In surviving pedimental compositions, no other goddess is as prominent or so frequently occupies the center.[37] An event in her life filled each gable of the Parthenon; on the east her birth was shown and on the west she competed with Poseidon for the possession of the land. Yet she is truly a male creation. She was born from the head of a male god, Zeus; she remained a virgin and war was one of her favorite pastimes. It is in the guise of an armed warrior-goddess that she is most frequently represented in monumental form. In short, it would not be easy or likely for an ordinary Athenian girl to identify with her.[38]

On the other hand, statues of young girls, *korai*, which adorned sanctuaries, especially the Acropolis at Athens during the archaic period, may have furnished such role models. Incredibly beautiful though they are, they nevertheless encourage shy behaviour, a willingness to serve, and modesty in dress.[39]

Until the middle of the fourth century, the female nude was rarely represented in Greek art. On the other hand, the male nude was a preponderant type in all art forms from the very beginning. This suggests that, in classical Greece, men enjoyed a superior status and a social freedom not granted to women. Thus, it was a new departure, indeed, when Praxiteles fashioned an undraped Aphrodite (Fig. 7) for the island of Knidos around 350 B.C., and to judge by the number and variety of sculptured nude goddesses which appear later in Hellenistic art, women's position had in the meantime significantly improved. Presumably, an ordinary Greek woman would yearn to resemble the beautiful naked object mounted on a pedestal and accompanied by Eros. But for both sexes, in a culture which so highly prized youth and good looks, it must have been hard to be old or malformed. Though, here again, men had the edge because at least their wisdom and dignity could increase with the years; old women were just fools.[40]

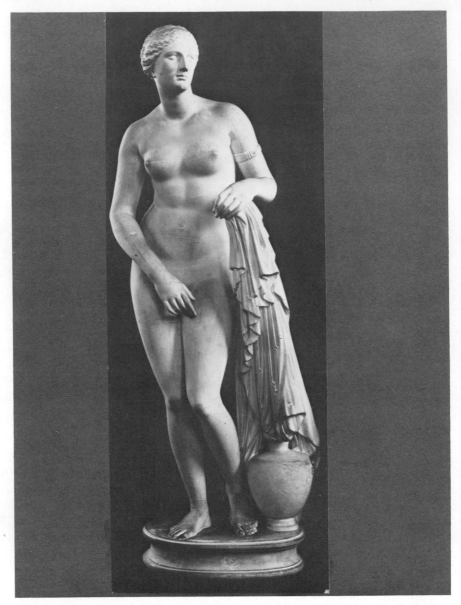

Fig. 7   Aphrodite of Knidos, by Praxiteles, Roman copy, Glyptothek, Munich

PART III: PRIVATE ART

When we turn to art in the private sector of Greek life, we become aware that the visual messages were less pointed and less likely to induce a given type of behaviour. One thinks first of vase painting. In the archaic and classical periods, the overwhelming number of representations on vases depict mythological subjects. While these cannot be dismissed simply as decoration any more than can the themes in architectural sculpture, their purpose here was educational rather than hortatory. They were intimate reminders, more personally conceived, of Greece's legendary past (Fig. 8). Perhaps we could call these mythological paintings on vases, so endlessly varied, an illustrated history. Some events depicted were major (such as the Trojan War), some were minor (the dressing of a warrior's wound). Sometimes the ridiculous side of life

Fig. 8   Herakles wrestling with Antaios, Krater signed by Euphronios, Paris, Louvre

is featured. But in general the scenes are rich in emotional range and they therefore fleshed out the restricted and always serious themes illustrated in monumental art.[41] They also conveyed much needed information. Perhaps the cloistered Greek mother could partially educate herself and her child by means of these domestic pots. Did they sometimes function, in short, as children's books?

It is interesting to note in this connection that, after 400, when general literacy had been established, the repertoire of myths on painted vases for domestic use begins to shrink markedly, and in the Hellenistic period it disappeared almost completely.[42]

Grave stelai are another category of art pertinent to our thesis. Archaic stelai in Attica are tall pillars with the deceased person depicted in relief; as monuments they are rare because extremely expensive.[43] After 450 they became rectangular in shape; in the fourth century they more and more came to resemble shrines.[44] Subject and content also change. In the sixth century, almost no women were commemorated; youthful warriors who died in battle monopolize the reliefs. In the fifth century, the actions are more informal but warriors continue to be celebrated and young women now make their entrance. However, the grave stelai of the fourth century are the most amazing. In official art of the period, as in the temple of Athena Alea at Tegea, the temple of Asklepios from Epidaurous or the Mausoleum friezes from Halikarnassos, standard battle themes and myths were continued. In Attic funerary art, on the other hand, after 400, husband and wife, children and servants assemble quietly and affectionately (Fig. 9). Two of them may clasp hands, but one cannot speak here of action or event. Sorrow is the real theme; it is felt by all those present and it unites them. The signals here are new: instead of the heroic ideal promoted in official art and summed up in the figure of Herakles, the grave stelai, privately commissioned, offer an alternative: membership in a family, in which solace and companionship are the rewards. An inevitable, but restrained, appeal is accordingly made to the passing spectator to contemplate another way of life.

While the art of any period or country conveys messages, the visual arts in ancient Greece were not as directive or didactic as those in many other cultures. The spectator was far less controlled as he walked around a sanctuary or street in Greece than he was at such locations in ancient or sixteenth century Rome, not to mention modern Paris or New York. Roads might ziz-zag and meander or, if straight, lead nowhere and reach no climax. Buildings would be competitive and unrelated, entrances and exits could be hard to find and one could keep tripping over small obstacles such as votive monuments, herms, treaty reliefs, statues, and open-air altars. Pausanias' descriptions can be exasperating to the archaeologist because he traverses the routes haphazardly, but assuredly this is the only way he could. The general impression would strike us today as disorderly, confused, and extremely untidy. Yet every individual object—temple, statue or vase—was in itself ordered, internally self-sufficient,

Fig. 9   Grave stele of Damasistrate, Athens, National Museum

and predictably designed. Perhaps it was the tension between these two competing impressions which determined, at least in part, the character of the Greek
race.

NOTES AND REFERENCES

[1] The most pertinent discussion is by T.B.L. Webster, *Classical Quarterly*, vol. 33,
1939, 166–179. Also illuminating are the three volumes by W. Miller, *Daedalus and
Thespis*; The Contributions of the Ancient Dramatic Poets to our knowledge of the
Arts and Crafts of Greece, New York, 1929–32.

[2] A recent and very useful book on "art" in Greece is J.J. Pollitt, *The Ancient View of
Greek Art*, New Haven, 1974. The translation of *techne* offered above is from Pollitt,
p. 32.

[3] Cf. E.A. Havelock, "Prologue to Greek Literacy," University of Cincinnati, *Classical
Studies* II, second series, 1966–71, 320 ff.

[4] Procopius, *Buildings*, I, 1, pp. 2–33. On the authenticity of Procopius' reaction: cf.
E.H. Swift, *Roman Sources of Christian Art*, New York, 1951, p. 209, n. 35.

[5] W.B. Dinsmoor, *American Journal of Archaeology*, 17, 1913, 53–80, 242–265,
371–398. J.J. Pollitt, *The Art of Greece, 1400–31 B.C.*, Prentice-Hall, New Jersey,
1965, 118–121.

[6] See Pollitt, *Ancient View*, 32–37.

[7] W. Miller, *Daedalus and Thespis*, 16.

[8] The Laocoon, today in the Vatican, is made of more than one piece of stone. But it
may not have been the version Pliny saw. The "Farnese Bull" is known only through
a rather grotesque copy in Naples.

[9] G.M.A. Richter, *Kouroi, Archaic Greek Youths*, Phaidon, 1960, Figs. 9–11.

[10] G.M.A. Richter, *Attic Red-Figured Vases*, New Haven, 1946, p. 51.

[11] *Ion*, Euripides, trans. A.P Burnett, Prentice-Hall, 1970.

[12] Compare R. Carpenter, *Greek Sculpture, A Critical Review*, Chicago, 1960, who
believes Greek sculptors became increasingly capable of surmounting the limitations
of human vision, and of achieving finally their ultimate goal of "mimetic fidelity."

[13] W. Miller, *Daedalus and Thespis*, 2, 335.

[14] J.J. Pollitt, *Art of Greece*, p. 203.

[15] Pliny's examples of works of art with powerful impact are mainly by artists of the
fourth century. Yet neither fourth-century painting or sculpture, known in copy or
original, can be justly labelled "realistic." On the contrary, they are still classical and
strongly idealized. Webster (note 1) overstresses the realism of Greek art in both the
fifth and fourth centuries. This is not uncommon.

[16] J.J. Pollitt, *Art of Greece*, p. 181.

[17] See R.M. Cook, *Greek Painted Pottery*, London, 1960, pp. 255–56.

[18] A perceptive account of narration in Greek art by G.M.A. Hanfmann can be found in
American Journal of Archaeology, 61, 1957, pp. 71ff. Also see E.H. Gombrich, *Art
and Illusion*, Pantheon Books, rev. ed. 1961, Part Two.

[19] See E.A. Havelock, *Preface to Plato,* Universal Library, 1967, p. 57, n. 22; J.J. Pollitt, *Ancient View of Greek Art,* pp. 37–41.

[20] Pollitt, *Ibid.,* pp. 41–50.

[21] Cf. G. Scott, *The Architecture of Humanism,* Doubleday, Anchor, 1954, Chapters VIII–IX; R. Carpenter, *Esthetic Basis of Greek Art,* Midland Book, Indiana University Press, 1959, pp. 137 ff.

[22] The significance of the gorgon or Medusa in particular is discussed in an interesting article, *Arion* 4, 1965, 484–494 by T.P. Feldman.

[23] Cf. R. Carpenter, *Esthetic Basis,* pp. 58 ff. On the language of gestures in the visual arts of Greece, see G. Neumann, *Gesten und Gebärden in der Griechischen Kunst,* Berlin, 1965.

[24] For the repertory of themes in pediments: E. Lapalus, *Le Fronton Sculpté en Grèce,* Paris, 1947, pp. 354 ff. For friezes: R. Demangel, *La frise Ionique,* Paris, 1932, pp. 365 ff.

[25] For example, The Dispute between Apollo and Herakles for the Delphic tripod was represented both in the East Pediment of the Treasury of the Siphnians and on an amphora by Phintias. (Illustrations: pediment, G.M.A. Richter, *A Handbook of Greek Art,* 4 ed., Phaidon, 1965, fig. 104; vase: P.E. Arias, *Greek Vase Painting,* Abrams, New York, n.d. fig. 92).

[26] As one would expect, battle scenes were also prominent in mural paintings. Pausanias describes scenes of this type in the Theseion and Painted Stoa in Athens (*Description,* I, 17, 2; I, 15, 1).

[27] For example, Centauromachy: Temple of Zeus, Olympia; Temple of Apollo, Bassae, Parthenon. Amazonomachy: Bassae, Parthenon, Gigantomachy: Temple of Artemis, Corfu, Hecatompedon II, Athens; Parthenon. Trojan War: Corfu, Temple of Aphaia, Aegina, Parthenon.

[28] Cf. E.A. Havelock, "War as a Way of Life in Classical Culture," *Classical Values and the Modern World,* The Vanier Lectures, Ottawa, Canada, 1970–71, 19ff. For the importance of struggle, contest or "agonia" in Greek society see V. Ehrenberg, *Polis und Imperium,* Zurich, 1965, pp. 339 f.

[29] Illustration of Parthenon, West Pediment: R.M. Cook, *Greek Art,* Noonday Press, 1972, fig. 47b.

[30] See Lapalus, *Op. cit.,* fig. 22.

[31] For a contrary opinion, see B. Ashmole, *Architect and Sculptor in Classical Greece,* Phaidon, 1972, pp. 29–40.

[32] Illustration for East Pediment: Lapalus, *Op. cit.,* fig. 32.

[33] The controversy about the meaning of the Parthenon frieze, its relation to the past and present, is summarized in R.R. Holloway, *A View of Greek Art,* Icon Edition, Harper and Row, 1974, pp. 125 ff.

[34] For a discussion of post-classical architectural sculpture, see C.M. Havelock, *Hellenistic Art,* New York, Graphic Society, pp. 185 ff.

[35] See D. von Bothmer, *Amazons in Greek Art,* Oxford, 1957.

[36] Illustrated in E. Schmidt, *The Great Altar of Pergamon,* Leipzig, 1962, Pls. 60–67.

[37] Only the gorgon or Medusa, the fantastic female monster, approaches Athena in popularity as the central motif.

[38] On the importance of Athena as goddess of Athens, see *Parthenos and Parthenon,* Oxford, 1963, G.T.W. Hooker, editor.

[39] The Korai are collected and well illustrated in G.M.A. Richter, Korai, *Archaic Greek Maidens*, Phaidon, 1968.

[40] The bearded philosopher of advanced age is a prominent type in the Hellenistic Age: Cf. M. Bieber, *Sculpture of the Hellenistic Age*, New York, rev. ed. 1961, figs. 230–242. There is nothing comparable for the opposite sex: see figs. 585 and 590 of Bieber, *ibid*.

[41] P.E. Arias, *Greek Vase Painting*, Abrams, New York, n.d. offers ample and attractive illustrations of Greek myths on painted vases.

[42] See R.M. Cook, *Greek Painted Pottery*, London, 1960, Chapters V, VI, VII.

[43] Cf. G.M.A. Richter, *The Archaic Gravestones of Attica*, Phaidon, 1961.

[44] Good illustrations of classical stelai can be found in K.F. Johansen, *The Attic Grave Reliefs*, Copenhagen, 1951, and H. Diepolder, *Die attischen Grabreliefs des 5 und 4 Jahrhunderts v. Chr.*, Berlin, 1931.

DR. EVA KEULS, who belongs to the current generation of "recycled housewives," is Professor of Classics at the University of Minnesota. Born in Amsterdam, Holland, she later came to the United States, and attended Hunter College, New York, where in one year she received her B.A. in Latin. Her graduate work was done at Columbia University, and in 1965 she received her Ph.D. Since then, she has had an active career in teaching and research, and has held several post-doctoral fellowships, including the prestigious Guggenheim (1974–75), and a year at the Netherlands Institute for Advanced Study (1976–77).

She has lectured and published on a variety of scholarly subjects: ancient rhetoric, the comedy of Menander, and mystic symbolism in Greek literature and art. Her book, *The Water Carriers in Hades* (Amsterdam 1974) traces the history of the myth of the Danaids in the classical literature and monuments, and presents a new reconstruction of the lost plays of Aeschylus' Danaid trilogy. Her most recent book, *Plato and Greek Painting* (Leiden 1977), a study of the philosopher's aesthetics, also proposes new interpretations of a number of Greek art-critical concepts.

Rhetoric and Visual Aids in Greece and Rome*

by EVA KEULS

T HE PURPOSE of this paper is to trace, through the literary sources of classical antiquity, the rhetorical device for which the Austrian scholar, O. Schissel von Fleschenberg, coined the name "Bildeinsatz"[1]—namely, that of introducing a discourse or story by a description of a painting, and to speculate that this practice was sometimes reinforced by the use of visual aids. Schissel rightly noted that this introductory convention is distinct from the descriptive

* Special abbreviations are listed at the end of this article.

digressions called *ekphraseis* which appear in the rhetorical handbooks of the first century A.D. and after, as well as in the creative literature of the Greco-Roman age. (The latter, as is well known, is to a considerable degree dependent on the rhetorical tradition.)[2]

In the "Bildeinsatz" technique the description is not digressive but proleptic—the painting described, often of a moralizing allegory, introduces the plot, theme or moral of the story or discourse to follow. Schissel studied the convention only as it manifests itself in the literature of the Greco-Roman age, from about 100 B.C. until the end of classical antiquity. He did not speculate on its origin and did not appear to be aware that the technique was rooted in the rhetorical practices of the Hellenic and early Hellenistic ages. I will here try to trace these roots.

The pursuit of skills in the art of persuasion probably goes back to the Mycenaean era (1600–1100 B.C.), but at least to centuries before the Classical Greek age. In the *Iliad* and the *Odyssey* one can find evidence that the Homeric heroes were well aware of the power of the spoken word and knew the conception of the "rhetor," the skilled public speaker.[3] The paragon of studied eloquence in the Homeric poems is Odysseus, the man "with the many wiles" (*polymēchanos*), as one of his epithets describes him.[4] In the *Iliad*, Odysseus is often selected for missions requiring tact and judgment, and many passages in both epics attest to his subtlety in presenting his case and to his persuasive power. His plea to Achilles to cease pouting and to return with his troop contingent to the battle line (*Il.* 9,225–306), though unsuccessful, is a well-composed speech of the type later classified as "deliberative" or political (*dēmēgorikos*). It includes two of the arguments later theoreticians are to list as standard categories for that type of speech, namely that of "honor" or glory (*timē*) and that of "expediency" (*to sympheron*).

An amusing passage in *Iliad* 3 reveals that Odysseus had developed a studied technique for delivery as well as compositional skill. The Trojan warrior Antenor had entertained both Menelaus and Odysseus in his mansion. He recalls that, when both were standing, Menelaus "with his broad shoulders" towered over his comrade. When both were seated, however, Odysseus was the more "lordly" (210–211). This is delicate wording, worthy of Odysseus himself, because it conveys the unflattering information that the hero's legs were too short. Yet, while addressing the assembly Odysseus knew how to overcome this handicap and to compete successfully against Menelaus' fluent, yet terse and lucid speeches. Odysseus, we learn, used to feign inarticulateness and fumble around until he had driven his audience to the edge of boredom. Then he recaptured them with a stream of words "coming down like snowflakes in winter" (222). By this rebound technique he made his listeners forget his unprepossessing stature and held them in the palm of his hand.[5]

The second major category of persuasive oratory, the courtroom speech, is not represented in the Homeric epic, but there is no reason to presume that it was not also already somewhat systematically developed. When, in the City of

Peace, embossed on the new shield of Achilles (*Il.* 18,490–508), we see two lit-
igants arguing over the blood-price in a murder case before a tribunal of elders,
we should probably imagine them doing this according to certain established
patterns. What is conspicuously absent in the Homeric epic is any vestige of
what in the Classical age emerges as the conventional third branch of rhetoric,
the epideictic (literally "showy") class, which does not aim at persuasion but
serves to enhance ceremonial occasions. The archetype of epideictic oratory
was probably the funeral eulogy. The major Classical exponent of this genre is
Pericles' funeral oration for the first Athenian dead of the Peloponnesian war,
as recreated by Thucydides (2,35–46). In Homer, although there are lavish
obsequies, we find no eulogies of the dead. At the funeral of Patroclus (*Il.*
23,108–897) only laments are uttered. The body of Hector is bewailed for nine
days before the funeral (*Il.* 24,665), but the warmest praise for the slain hero is
conveyed, as so often in the epic, by implication. The last dirge for Hector is
that by Helen, now widely resented by the Trojans—she laments that only
Hector had been gentle with her (771–772).

If courtroom and political oratory are designed to persuade, the funeral
eulogy may at least be said to aim at conviction, since the speaker tries to convey the impression that the deceased has not lived and died in vain. When,
however, epideictic rhetoric emerges as a fully developed (if always peripheral)
third branch of the discipline in the late fifth and early fourth centuries B.C., it
has lost even this semblance of utility. The eulogy has now been expanded into
the encomium, not just of the recently deceased but of anything and anybody.[6]
The encomium becomes the byword for rhetoric for the sake of rhetoric (Plato,
Symposium 177 b), a literary genre on the borderline between oratory and
belles lettres, designed to entertain or to dazzle rather than to instruct or to
move to action. So far has the genre strayed from even the pretense of conviction that, for virtuoso effect, it often seeks out topics notoriously unworthy of
praise. So we know of an Encomium of Mice (Polycrates) and one of Death
(Alcidamas).[7] Among the few published and extant encomia there is one entitled "The Praise of Helen," attributed, probably correctly, to the fifth-century
rhetorician Gorgias.[8] This is actually not so much a eulogy of Helen—her legendary assets, beauty and seductiveness, are slighted—as an apologue against an
implied accusation of adultery. As Gomperz has rightly stressed, the argumentation developed could be applied to any remotely similar case and, in effect,
tends to establish, not the innocence of Helen, but the notion that adultery is
never culpable.[9] That this display of resourcefulness is not intended in a serious
vein, is revealed by the author himself who refers to his composition as a "jest"
(*paignion*, 21). From the hand of Isocrates we also have a "Praise of Helen,"
actually a critique of Gorgias and other encomium writers who waste their time
on such undeserving topics as bumblebees and salt (*ibid*. 12).[10]

The extant encomia from the Classical Greek age do not contain extensive
descriptions of any kind: the evidence for such, to be outlined below, pertains
to compositions of which no full texts survive. Before turning to their vestiges,

however, I propose to look briefly at the rhetorical theory, insofar as it deals with descriptive language. Of the vast technical literature on rhetoric produced during the Hellenic age, only Aristotle's treatise *On Rhetoric* survives. This work has a pronounced pragmatic bias: it concentrates on courtroom and political oratory and neglects the epideictic branch. It did, however, give rise to a peculiar confusion of terminology in regard to descriptive language, which apparently grew out of a misinterpretation of Aristotle's wording. In the *Rhetoric*, under the rubric of style (*lexis*), Aristotle recommends *energeia*, a difficult term sometimes rendered as "actuality" or "actualization," but in a rhetorical context meaning approximately "forceful description of an action". Aristotle defines it once as "the placing of things before the eyes" (3,11,2) and once as "movement" (*kinēsis* 3,11,4). The rhetorical literature of the Hellenistic age is almost entirely lost. From the Greco-Roman age, however, a considerable body of technical literature is extant in both Greek and Latin, and by now virtually all forms of composition in prose have found a place under the heading of rhetoric. Among the extensive technical vocabulary for purely descriptive passages, developed in this later literature, we find the frequently recurrent term *enargeia*, "visual vividness," as a desirable quality of style for such digressions. In the handbooks on preliminary exercises (*progymnasmata*), *enargeia* represents the keynote of the principal type of descriptive digression, the *ekphrasis*, which deals with static objects and places.[11]

The two terms *energeia* and *enargeia* are not related etymologically. The former comes from the root -erg-, "work", and has given us the derivative "energy". The latter is derived from the adjective *argos*, "clear," and means brightness, lucidity and, by extension, visual vividness (as e.g. in Plato, *Statesman* 277 b). In the Greco-Roman rhetorical literature, however, a contamination of the two terms took place. In the Greek texts they are used interchangeably[12] and in the Latin translations of *enargeia* the notions of "lucidity," "visual vividness" and "forcefulness" are intermingled in confusion.

Quintilian gives three different accounts of the meaning of *enargeia*:

a). In 4,2,63–64, *evidentia* (to be classified under the rubric of *perspicuitas*)
b). In 6,2,32 (quoting Cicero): *illustratio* and *evidentia*
c). In 8,3,61, *evidentia* and *repraesentatio* (rather than *perspicuitas*)

In passage a). Quintilian admits to uncertainty about the meaning of the term ("as far as I for one understand"); the third comment contradicts the first. The key passage for the confusion between the notions is the second, 6,2,32. Here Quintilian notes that *enargeia* is the faculty which causes us "not so much to say as to show things,"[13] it brings out "emotions" (*adfectus*). As examples he cites passages from the *Aeneid* which constitute colorful narrations of actions, not descriptive digressions. His paradigms are comparable to the passages from Euripides and Homer cited by Aristotle to illustrate his feature of *energeia* in *Rhetoric* 3,11. It appears that Aristotle's notion of "forcefulness" was transformed into a quality of style appropriate for stationary themes as a result of the accidental similarity of the two terms and also, perhaps, by virtue of a general trend of later Greek aesthetic thought to convert originally dynamic conceptions into static ones.

Aristotle's *Rhetoric*, then, makes no allusion to purely graphic language, nor does it yield any indication that the rhetorical practices of his time included extended descriptions. The earliest trace of a visual approach in rhetoric, however, antedates Aristotle by about a century: it is found in the reports on what appears to have been the most popular lecture delivered in the Classical age, a discourse entitled "The Praise of Heracles" by Prodicus of Ceos.[14] Prodicus was a contemporary and, perhaps, sometime associate of Socrates and one of the most important figures of the second generation of sophists. Prodicus went on a tour of the Greek cities with his lecture and harvested so much success with it that his performance was remembered until late antiquity.[15] Whether the text was published we do not know, but Xenophon (*Memorabilia* 2,1,22) has left us a short account of it.

Prodicus described Heracles at the crossroads of Vice and Virtue; female impersonations of these were beckoning to him along either path and, after due deliberation, he chose the latter. Xenophon's account makes it clear that Prodicus used very graphic language and tried to evoke in the minds of his listeners a visual impression of the two ladies, their attire and the enticements they held out to Heracles. I will cite only the description of Vice:

> The other was overnourished to the point of obesity and flabbiness, but dolled up with color, so as to appear both whiter and redder than she was in reality; her posture was unnaturally erect, her eyes opened brazenly; her dress was such as to reveal most clearly the bloom of her youth.

Xenophon claims to cite Prodicus from memory and, indeed, the baroque style is not his own.[16]

Prodicus' allegory of the "forked road" was not original (see e.g. Hesiod, *Works and Days* 287–292). The image is usually associated with the Pythagoreans, who expressed it pictorially through the symbol of the letter Y. The entire stress on visual imagery, in fact, appears to hark back to the Pythagorean school. Proclus, in his essay *On Plato's Theology*, distinguishes the Orphic way of communicating "divine things" through "symbols," akin to "divine tales" (*theomythiai*), from that of the Pythagoreans, who did so by means of "pictures" (*eikones*).[17]

That Prodicus illustrated his lecture by displaying an actual painting or drawing of his motif is not indicated by the sources. One late reference, however, suggests that a well-known painting on the theme existed.[18] It is, of course, possible that such a painting was inspired by Prodicus' famous lecture, but the reverse is more probable.

Before we leave the Classical Greek age, we might point out that the use of painted aids for occasions other than rhetorical is well attested for that era. This is an altogether natural phenomenon, as painting, a latecomer among the fine arts of Greece, underwent an explosive development during the fifth century (of which, unfortunately, we must trace the phases mainly from literary sources) and soon pervaded all phases of public and private life. Public buildings were lavishly decorated with wall paintings, two halls of the Propylaea on the Acropolis of Athens were designed as painting galleries, and in one city, Sicyon, the art of painting was even integrated into a system of universal higher education (Pliny, *Natural History* 35,77). As is well-known, Sophocles is credited with the introduction of painted props as backdrops for the theater and literary sources have recorded the name of the first major "scene painter" (*skēnographos*), Agatharchus.

Another, less well attested but nevertheless probable use of painted props occurred in the celebration of some mysteries. The highest grade of initiation required the experience of "vision" (*epopteia*). Vision of what? In the case of the Greater Eleusinian Mysteries "vision" was undoubtedly that of certain sacred objects, perhaps genitalia and other symbols of fertility and possibly, although this is disputed, of dramas. An important fragment of Plutarch, however, also alludes to the showing of "sacred sites," signifying the Elysean fields into which the initiant moves symbolically after his initiation in life and for which he is headed after death:

> . . . and after this (i.e. the terrors of initiation) a wondrous light came at them and sacred places and meadows were shown. [19]

The source, like all of the more concrete allusions to initiation procedure, is late, but nevertheless likely to record authentic tradition as Plutarch was an initiate himself. In what form were "the sacred places and meadows" shown? Nothing but painted walls or panels comes to mind that could have served the purpose.

Because Prodicus was a sophist and surely dedicated to the denial of moral absolutes, we must assume that his "Praise of Heracles," in spite of the moralizing nature of the theme, was not meant to edify but to entertain and impress.[20] In the Stoic school of philosophy the allegorical approach to mythological themes becomes a matter of dogma, but now the allegory serves earnest moralizing purposes. In format, however, the homilies recited by the Stoics seem to be modeled on those of Prodicus, except that the ties with painted representations are now more concrete. So Cicero reports of the Stoic Cleanthes, pupil and successor of the school's founder, Zeno, that he used to describe an allegorical painting of Pleasure (*Voluptas*) to which the Virtues had surrendered themselves as handmaidens (*De Finibus* 2,21). Cleanthes, Cicero states, used "to paint the painting with words." He "invited his listeners to imagine (*cogitare*) with him Pleasure painted on a panel . . ." The verb *cogitare* makes it clear that the process was purely mental and did not entail the display of an actual painting. The conceit, however, was carried through at some length because Cleanthes qualifies his explanation with the words "if only one would be able to read the painting in this way."[21]

For Cleanthes' pupil Chrysippus a written description of a painting is attested by Diogenes Laertius (7,187–188). In his work *On the Ancient Natural Philosophers*, Chrysippus told a story of Zeus and Hera, which Diogenes censures as obscene "even though the author praised it as being in conformance with nature."[22] That Chrysippus' treatment of the theme had the format of the description of a painting is shown by Diogenes' subsequent remark that it departed from the versions recorded in Polemon, Hypsicrates and Antigonus (Polemon and Antigonus are well-established art-historical sources).[23] Diogenes apparently did not believe that the description was based on an actual painting, but the reference to the same treatise in Origen (*supra* n. 22) reveals that the latter did. Origen, in fact, reports the painting's location: according to him it was kept on the island of Samos.

A visually evocative technique, therefore, is well attested for the Stoic lecturers and authors.[24] The only clear evidence, however, for the use of an actual visual aid, is found in the domain of political oratory: Pliny the Elder (*Natural History* 35,23) reports that L. Hostilius Mancinus, the first Roman to enter Carthage after its surrender, set up pictures representing "the site and the attacks on it" and explained them to the populace in the Forum while campaigning for the consulate.

Whether or not we should imagine the itinerant Greek rhetors of the Hellenic and early Hellenistic ages as traveling with paintings or reproductions in their luggage, their practice of starting a discourse with the description of a painting had a profound influence on the literature of the Greco-Roman age. The technique developed into a standard literary device, best represented in the rhetorical literature of the second century A.D. (the age often referred to as the Second Sophistic) and in the Greek and Latin romances; occasionally it is adapted to poetry as well. No Greek or Latin terms for it are known, hence Schissel's expression "Bildeinsatz" (*supra* n. 1) is not a translation.

Of the rhetorical literature of the Second Sophistic we might cite Lucian's *Slander* as an example. The author starts his discourse with the description of an allegory on his subject, painted by Apelles. Lucian also cites the incident in the painter's life which allegedly inspired him to depict this theme. The incident is clearly spurious[25] and the entire painting may have existed only in Lucian's imagination.

The device of labeling a fictitious allegory as the work of a famous painter is worked into a literary conceit by Lucian in *On Salaried Posts in Great Houses*. The speaker illustrates the life of those who have surrendered to greed with an allegory of Wealth. He "wishes to paint a picture of such a one's life just as that certain Cebes does." Gladly, he says, he would enlist the services of an Apelles, Parrhasius, Aëtion or Euphranor, but, as in his time no one of comparable nobility and skill is to be found, he will "present the painting bare in his epideictic speech, as best he can" (*psilēn ōs oion te soi epideixō tēn eikona*).

Often the technique entails an interpreter of the painting other than the author. In such cases the persona of the interpreter or exegete intervenes between that of the author and those of characters of the principal theme or action. Most typically, the first narrator comes upon the interpreter by chance. The feature of the interpreter, who stands outside the principal action, leans to the technique of "Bildeinsatz" a didactic and moralizing tone which in itself is sufficient to set it apart from general descriptive digressions in literature.

In the discourse *Pinax* ("Painting") by Pseudo-Cebes (cf. the Cebes mentioned by Lucian in the passage cited above), an allegory on the different ways of life, dating from the beginning of our era, but composed in the earlier Pythagorean-Stoic tradition, the conceit of the painted scene is maintained throughout and the interpreter's didactic role is constantly recalled.[26]

The feature of the accidental meeting of the principal persona and the interpreter also lends to the device a factor of chance, which makes it especially suitable for the romances where Tyche or Fortuna reigns: hence, no doubt, the elaborate applications of the scheme in Achilles Tatius and Longus. That the coincidence theme is by now pure conventional plot machinery is obvious in Achilles Tatius, because this author duplicates it. The first persona comes upon the painting (of Europa and the bull) by accident and casually strikes up a conversation with another chance onlooker, Clitophon, who then becomes the narrator of the tale. At the end of the work Achilles Tatius forgets to tie up his loose ends and the first persona never re-appears.

As Schissel noted (*supra* n. 1, p. 109), the technique, when applied to the romances, reveals yet another convention, namely a lament on the power of Eros;[27] the paintings in these instances represent love scenes and set the stage for the romantic aspect of the story. The entire technique is hilariously spoofed by Petronius, that tireless satirist of literary cliches.[28] The narrator of his story, Encolpius, has been deserted by his boy-friend Giton and wanders through a picture gallery to find distraction from the sorrows of love. Inevitably, however, his eyes wander to paintings depicting the pederastic dalliances of the gods and he utters the traditional lament: "So even the gods are touched by love," (83,10). He then meets the poet Eumolpus, a mouthpiece of literary conventions, who soon feels called upon to deliver himself of a homily on greed, a conventional bawdy Milesian tale and a miniature epic in Vergilian style on the capture of Troy. His pretext for the Trojan *epyllion* is his listener's supposed interest in a painting on the topic:[29] "But I see that you have eyes only for that painting which shows the capture of Troy; so I will try to expand on the work with my verse." (89,1–3) The joke, of course, lies in the incongruity of the theme and Encolpius' mood and personality.

That a technique which originated in the didactic homilies of the Pythagoreans and Stoics found such a ready home in the fictional prose literature of the Greco-Roman age should not cause surprise—it was made to order for the quasi-moralizing tone of the Greek and Latin romances.[30]

The above survey shows that the evocation of a visual image, usually a painting, as a pretext to introduce a discourse or narrative, had a continuous history in the rhetorical tradition and that it profoundly influenced the creative literature of the Greco-Roman age.[31] Yet in only one case, that of L. Hostilius Mancinus, did our sources make it evident that a public speaker actually set up a painting or drawing as an aid in communication. The question nevertheless arises whether in the preliminary stages of education, intended to form future citizens eminent in the prized skills of rhetoric, such aids were used. On the basis of the literary evidence alone the answer would have to be negative. In the collections of *progymnasmata* from the Imperial period, descriptive exercises are recommended (under the heading of *ekphrasis*), but only marginally and solely for the sake of historiography, now subsumed under rhetoric (Theon, in Spengel II, 60,20–21). Accordingly, students are to practise such composition by imitating descriptive passages in famous historians (*ibid.* II, 68; 118; 46; cf. n. 2 *supra*).

The pragmatic Quintilian is somewhat less tolerant of the "poetic licence" of the historians (2,4,3), but at times condones descriptions as useful for some types of composition (4,2,123; 9,2,41–44). Nowhere, however, is there any mention of the use of visual objects or scenes as the basis for such exercises. The essence of rhetorical and literary education, in Quintilian's conception, is the paraphrase of poetry and the emulation of canonical authors.

Similarly, when Hermogenes in his essay on literary composition (*De ideis*) recommends practice in the description of idyllic spots, he does not send his pupils to the painting galleries to look at sacro-idyllic scenes or to the groves and gardens themselves, but to the description of the resting place under the planetree in Plato's *Phaedrus* (230 b–c) and other famous idylls in standard literature (p. 331, 17–24, ed. Rabe).

The monuments, on the other hand, make it clear that persons who received a liberal arts education, were by no means deprived of visual inspiration. The repetitiveness of Greco-Roman iconography in wall painting indicates that collections of reproductions were in circulation for the benefit of graphic artists.[32] There were illustrated editions, at least of Greek New Comedy and the plays of Terence, and probably of other literary works as well.[33] (Thus far, none are attested earlier than the first century A.D.) Without much doubt a text illustrated with pictures of key scenes served as the model for the recently published mosaics of the House of Menander at Mytilene on the island of Lesbos.[34]

That any such standard pictorial aids were used in rhetorical practice, either for the perpetuation of the technique of "Bildeinsatz" or for any other descriptive composition, is not indicated by the evidence presently available. There is, however, a small class of surviving graphic monuments which appears to have served some educational purpose; I refer to the so-called Homeric tablets.[35] These are a group of 19 marble plaques, decorated in low relief with motifs from Homer and other heroic episodes. Most of the themes are accompanied by an explanatory inscription in Greek, an extract, gloss or paraphrase, or an epigram on the subject.

All tablets of which the provenance is fairly certain were found in the vicinity of Rome and they date from different phases of the Roman Imperial period. Although the destination of the tablets is by no means clear, there are indications in the texts of the inscriptions that they served an educational purpose. Strongest suggestion of school use comes from the tablets numbered 1 and 2 by Sadurska. These two tablets belong to a group of five whose manufacture is ascribed to one Theodorus because they bear his signature. The first two of these show, on the rim of the tablet, an exhortation to the reader in elegiac meter to "study the art of Theodorus, so that, having learned the structure of Homer, you may have a measure of all wisdom."[36]

Scholars who have other notions about the purpose of the tablets (alternative theories favor either a cultic or a decorative use) raise objections to the scholastic thesis, of which some appear more impressive than others.[37] The observation that there are spelling errors in the Greek texts reveals a touching regard for the teaching profession, but it does not provide a valid argument against the assumption that the tablets were used in schools.[38] The objection that the scenes include some indecent ones seems anachronistic: after all, walls uncovered in Pompeii, including some of family dining rooms, are decorated with scenes of explicit sex. More valid is the argument that the tablets are small for classroom use (the two largest ones measure 25 x 40 and 20 x 29 cm). On some (notably Sadurska nr. 4, "The Shield of Achilles") the script is so small that it is barely legible with the naked eye.

The argument cannot be discussed in detail here, but at least it can be said that, whereas some doubts about the pedagogic thesis remain, the latter is intrinsically far more probable than the assumption that the tablets served as ex-voto's (Schefold) or as wall decorations for private villas (Sadurska).

If these tablets did, indeed (as seems likely to this writer), serve as mnemonic devices, to aid children in memorizing the basic myths and literary passages of their culture through pictorial representations, they constitute the only known visual aids in ancient education. We owe the preservation of the 19 tablets to the circumstance that marble, though fragile, is imperishable. We should probably assume that similar illustrated materials were produced on other, perishable materials such as papyrus, parchment and wood. The Homeric tablets, as well as the general close correspondence of the literary and the fine arts in the classical world make it highly likely that ancient education was more visually oriented than the literary-rhetorical handbooks would indicate.

NOTES AND REFERENCES

SPECIAL ABBREVIATIONS

Gomperz, *Sophistik und Rhetorik*: H. Gomperz, *Sophistik und Rhetorik, Das Bildung-sideal des Eu Legein in seinem Verhältnis zur Philosophie des* V. *Jahrhunderts*, Berlin-Leipzig 1912

Kroll, *Rhetorik*: Wilhelm Kroll, "Rhetorik", *Realenzyklopädie der Altertumswissenschaft, Supplementband VII* (1940), 1039–1138

Lausberg, *Handbuch*: Heinrich Lausberg, *Handbuch der literarischen Rhetorik*, Munich 1960

Spengel: *Rhetores Graeci*, ed. L. Spengel, Leipzig 1853 (repr. 1966)

[1] "Die Technik des Bildeinsatzes", *Philologus* 72 (1913) 83–114.

[2] *Ekphrasis* is included among the *progymnasmata*, preliminary rhetorical exercises, of the Imperial age. The earlier handbooks on *progymnasmata* (Theon, Hermogenes and Aphthonius, all in Spengel) did not explicitly include works of art as suitable topics. Statues and paintings first appear as *ekphrasis* themes in the *Progymnasmata* of Nicolaos (5th century A.D.), Spengel III, 492, 11–12. "Bildeinsatz" and *ekphrasis* thus represent two separate traditions.

[3] Homer, *Iliad* 9,443 uses the term *rhētēr*, "speaker" or "teller of tales". The word *rhētōr* is first attested in the latter half of the fifth century B.C.

[4] Another epithet, *polymētis*, "many-counseled," has approximately the same implications.

[5] Quintilian, 12,10,64 associates the principal Homeric orators with the traditional three styles in rhetoric—Menelaus represents the plain, Nestor the intermediate, and Odysseus the grand style.

[6] Following Aristotle, *Rhetoric* 1.3.3 and 1,9,1, epideictic oratory is sometimes subdivided into "praise" and "censure" (cf. Quintilian 3,7,1), although the latter can hardly constitute an independent genre. (Censure may, however, be featured as part of epideictic composition, as Aristotle points out, *ibidem* 3,14,2.) That epideictic oratory consisted mainly of praise is shown by the fact that in later rhetorical theory it was known alternately as "the panegyric genre" (*genos panēgyrikon*).

[7] According to Cicero, *Tusculan Disputations* 1,48,116, the latter consisted mainly of an enumeration of the ills of life. If so, it anticipated the post-Hellenic consolation literature; see Gomperz, *Sophistik und Rhetorik* 109–110.

[8] H. Diels, *Fragmente der Vorsokratiker* II, 288–294.

[9] *Sophistik und Rhetorik* 11–12.

[10] Later rhetorical theory, following Isocrates, *Helen* 1, designates such praises of unworthy objects as "paradoxical encomia"; see Menander Rhetor, Spengel III, 346,10.

[11] Spengel II, 16, 46 and 118. In an anonymous rhetorical treatise of the Greco-Roman age the term *enargeia* is used, not for a quality of *ekphrasis* but for the device itself (Spengel II, 439, 10–11). (On "visual vividness" as a quality of prose style see Kroll, *Rhetorik* 111–1112.) In Demetrius, *On Style* 209 and Ps.-Longinus, *On the Sublime* 15,2 we find definitions of *enargeia* which echo the notions of "movement" and "forcefulness" inherent in the Aristotelian *energeia*.

[12] In a treatise providing a definition of *ekphrasis* otherwise paralleling that of Theon (*infra* n. 13) the adverb *energōs* is used instead of the customary *enargōs*, Spengel III. 251, 25–26. In fact, in Spengel's index, *loci* for both *enargeia* and *energeia* are listed under the latter entry. The Latin translations show that the confusion does not stem from spelling errors but that a contamination of ideas took place.

[13] The common notion of "placing things before the eyes" held together the two otherwise distinct concepts: Aristotle, *Rhetorik* 3,11,1: "to place before the eyes" (*energeia*). Theon, *Progymnasmata*, Spengel II, 118, 6–9: "*Ekphrasis* is a descriptive passage which sets its subject vividly (*enargōs*) before the eyes". Quintilian 8,3,62: "(things are) shown to the eyes of the mind" (*enargeia*).

[14] This is the title suggested by Plato, *Symposium* 177 b.

[15] See H. Diels, *Fragmente der Vorsokratiker* II, 308–312 for the sources. The dialogue between Just and Unjust Discourse in Aristophanes' *Clouds* 889 ff. appears to be based on Prodicus' speech (see the mention of Prodicus in 361). Cf. *Birds* 692, which reveals that Prodicus also lectured on the nature of the gods.

[16] Cf. the amusing incident in Plato's *Protagoras* 316a, where Prodicus, though ill and in bed, fills the room with such "booming" (*bombos*) that no one understands a word.

[17] The word *eikones*, like the English "images," is ambiguous; it may refer to verbal images as well as to actual pictures. The antithesis in the sentence indicates that Proclus here means the latter. The Pythagoreans' scorn for verbal communication and the mandatory silence (*echemythia*) they imposed on their followers are widely attested (see e.g. Plutarch, *Table Talk* 8,8,2).

[18] Philostratus, *Life of Apollonius of Tyana* 6,10. A "naked philosopher" (gymnosophist) introduces his own description of "Heracles at the Crossroads" as follows: "Surely you saw, in discourses on painting (*en zōgraphias logois*), the Heracles of Prodicus." The passage, though ambiguous, suggests an illustrated description of an actual painting.

[19] The passage, cited in Stobaeus, *Florilegium* 4,107, is generally thought to derive from Plutarch's lost essay *On the Soul*. See N. Turchi, *Fontes Historiae Mysteriorum Aevi Hellenistici*, Rome 1930, 81–82. The reference is not to the Greater Eleusinian Mysteries, since no ordeals of initiation are attested for these. Perhaps it applies to the preliminary Lesser Mysteries at Agrai near Athens, which were dominated by the figures of Dionysus and Pan and which had a bucolic flavor.

[20] Cicero, *On the Nature of the Gods* 1,118, rebukes Prodicus for the absence of true morality (*religio*) in his allegories: "So Prodicus of Ceos, who said that all things which are of benefit to man should be numbered among the gods, what morality did he leave behind?"

[21] In Cicero, *Tusculan Disputations* 5,4,14, there is an oblique allusion to a painted allegory of the Virtues (also in connection with Stoic lecturing practices). On the meaning of the verb *intellegere* in connection with paintings see *infra* n. 31.

[22] The myth was that of the sacred marriage of Zeus and Hera, as Origen, *Contra Celsum* 4,48, reports (H. von Arnim, *Stoicorum Veterum Fragmenta*, Leipzig 1905, 2 nr. 1074, p. 314).

[23] "Hypsicrates" should probably be emended into "Xenocrates" to conform with Pliny, *Natural History* 35,68: ". . Antigonus and Xenocrates who wrote about painting." So U. von Moellendorff-Wilamowitz, *Antigonos von Karistos*², Berlin-Zürich 1965, 8. Hence the Greek *pinakes* in 188 means "paintings" and not "lists of titles" as rendered by R.D. Hicks in the Loeb edition.

[24] A curious passage in Philodemus' fragmentary essay *On Poems* may recall the didactic

nature of such visually evocative passages, at least in Stoic contexts. The Epicurean philosopher of the first century A.D. cites an opposing opinion, almost certainly one of Stoic orientation, according to which "a good poet must delight his hearers but benefit those who see" (*De poematis*, ed. Chr. Jensen, Fr. II, p. 7, 24–27). Jensen, 123, offers a different explanation of the lines.

25 The revolt of Theodotus against Ptolemy IV (ruled 221–204 B.C.), which is the basis of the story, took place a century after the days of Apelles.

26 See Robert Joly, *Le Tableau de Cébès et la philosophie religieuse*, Brussels 1963, where older literature may be found. As Joly, 59–60, rightly points out, the interpreter motif is here intertwined with the theme of the indoctrination of the young by the old—the interpreter had in his youth received the explanation from the donor (someone "zealously pursuing a Pythagorean or Parmenidean life") and is passing it on in his old age. The indoctrination theme constitutes one of the many ties between the discourse and mystery or initiation symbolism. Other instances of the interpreter feature: Petronius, *Satyricon* 81–88; Lucian, *Toxaris* 6 and *Heracles* 4–6; Ps.-Lucian, *Amores* 8; Longus, *Daphnis and Chloe*, proem.

27 Petronius 83,10; Achilles Tatius 1,2,1; Longus, Proem 2.

28 On Petronius as a satirist of literary clichés see Richard Heinze, "Petron und der griechische Roman", *Hermes* 34 (1899) 494–519; E. Courtney, "Parody and Literary Allusion in Menippean Satire", *Philologus* 106 (1962) 86–100.

29 The "Bildeinsatz" technique is applied in the Aeneid itself as well. The description of a painting depicting the Trojan battles (1,455–493) foreshadows the account of the fall of Troy in book II. See Hans Jucker, *Vom Verhältnis der Römer zu der bildenden Kunst der Griechen*, Frankfurt 1950, 177–178, where the connection of the description with the theme of the epic is discussed. For an interpretation of the motif of the Danaids on the baldric of Pallas as "Bildeinsatz" see Eva Keuls, *The Water Carriers in Hades: A Study of Catharsis through Toil in Classical Antiquity*, Amsterdam 1974, 115–116.

30 As noted, Schissel, who coined the term "Bildeinsatz," did not speculate on the origin of this convention. Erwin Rohde, *Der griechische Roman und seine Vorläufer* [3], Leipzig 1914, 360, n. 3, following Fr. Matz, *De Philostratorum in describendis imaginibus fide*, Diss. Bonn 1867, 7 ff., denies the connection between the description of paintings and the moralizing allegories of the philosophers. Nor did Paul Friedländer, *Johannes von Gaza und Paulus Silentiarius*, Leipzig 1912, 83–103, surveying rhetorical art descriptions in Greek and Latin literature, note a connection with Prodicus and the early Stoics.

31 We are here concerned only with the proleptic descriptions of paintings, not with those which are integrated into literature in other ways, nor with descriptions as an independent literary genre (except for the *Pinax* by Pseudo-Cebes). For the Roman pride in the art of the "interpretation" of a painting, known as *intellegere* (Cicero, *De Finibus* 2,21; Petronius 52,3; Pliny, *Natural History* 34,77 and 35,98; Quintilian 12,10,3) see Keuls, *op. cit.* (*supra* n. 43) 113–114. For the traditional use of descriptions other than of paintings in proems, see O. Schissel von Fleschenberg, *Novellenkränze Lucians*, Halle a.S. 1912, 15 and 61–62.

32 Kurt Weitzmann, *Ancient Book Illumination*, Cambridge, Mass. 1959, 3, speculates that "picture cycles in books" served as the sources of conventional iconographic schemes. Karl Schefold, *Vergessenes Pompeji*, Bern and Munich 1962, 44 and 78, speaks of "picture books" (Bilderbücher).

[33] For an illustrated fragment of New Comedy from the first or second century A.D. (Florence papyrus PSI 847) see Weitzmann, *op. cit.* (n. 47 *supra*) 64 and V. Bartoletti, *Studi Italiani di Filologia Classica* 34 (1962) 21–25; for an unpublished fragment of a prose text in Paris (Bibliothèque Nationale nr. 1294), perhaps of a romance, Weitzmann, *ibidem* 100 and Fig. 107. Oxyrhynchus papyri 2652 and 2653, dating from the second or third century A. D., are fragments of an illustrated Menander text.

[34] See S. Charitonidis, L. Kahil and R. Ginouvès, *Les Mosaïques de la Maison du Ménandre à Mytilène*, Bern 1970, 102–105.

[35] See Anna Sadurska, *Les Tables iliaques*, Warsaw 1964, for full illustrations and older literature.

[36] Sadurska p. 29, lines b 1–2; similarly p. 39, lines b 1–2.

[37] The arguments and pertinent bibliography are presented in Sadurska 18–19.

[38] Cf. Eric G. Turner, *Greek Manuscripts of the Ancient World*, Oxford 1971, 32 and Plate 4, for a spelling error in the teacher's paradigm on a school boy's wood-and-wax writing tablet.

BRUNO GENTILI is Professor of Greek literature at the University of Urbino, Italy, and editor of the journal, *Quaderni Urbinati di cultura classica*, as well as other series of texts and critical essays. He himself has also contributed to Italian and foreign journals. His cultural and philological interests are focussed primarily on the study of Archaic Greece, and among his major works in this area are studies of Bacchylides and Simonides; a critical edition, with introduction and translation, of Anacreon; and a commentary on the Greek lyric poets in the well-known volume, *Polinnia*. He has also devoted two volumes to the systematic study of Greek metrics, a subject in which he is now one of the outstanding specialists. He is also among those who urge the application of a new methodology to the study of the ancient world, a methodology that is in harmony with the cultural directions of our time; see, for example, his study on the archaic and late archaic Greek lyric in *Introduzione allo studio della cultura classica*, Milan, 1972. His other recent publications are also numerous: *Le teorie del discorso storico nel penisero greco e la storiografia romana arcaica* (with G. Cerri), Rome, 1976; *Storia della letteratura latina* (with E. Pasoli and M. Simonetti), Rome-Bari, 1976; and *Lo spettacolo nel mondo antico*, Rome-Bari, 1977.

GIOVANNI CERRI is Assistant Professor of Greek and Latin Philology at the University of Urbino, and is also charged with the teaching of Greek literature at the *Istituto Universitario Orientale* of Naples. In the course of his research, he has been especially concerned with political language in archaic Greek lyric poetry and in Greek tragedy. Among his more important works are a study of the use of political language in the *Prometheus* of Aeschylus (Rome, 1975), and a volume, written in collaboration with B. Gentili, on Greek and early Roman historical thought (Rome, 1975).

Written and Oral Communication in Greek Historiographical Thought[1]

by B. GENTILI and G. CERRI

Le privilège que la théorie de la science a accordé
à l'histoire, depuis l'entrée en scène de la
dialectique materielle, semble avoir provisoirement
omis une évidence: que l'histoire est narration,
est language *rapportant*.

JEAN PIERRE FAYE, *Languages totalitaires*, Paris 1972

IT HAS BEEN observed that the discovery of the historical dimension of man
was, for the Greeks, a poetic one[2]; as early as the seventh century B.C. the
elegiac poet Mimnermus of Colophon, narrating the colonization of his native
town and the wars which followed it, interpreted the misadventures of the
present as expiation of ancient guilt, according to a principle of divinely imposed causality which tended to re-establish order in human affairs.[3] More generally, a recurrent element in archaic Greek poetry was the recounting of
remote history together with recent and even contemporary events (the coloni-

137

zation of cities, wars, civil and political strife) in which, at times, the poet himself had been a protagonist with a strongly partisan spirit. This was a pragmatic
poetry, directly involved in the real problems of its own society but, at the same
time, seeking to indicate its political-historical antecedents by recalling the
past. [4] The sense of difference and the awareness of continuity—the two basic
components of historical thought—were in fact, as the poetry of Homer and
Hesiod clearly shows, already an acquired element of archaic Greek culture in
its bi-polar conception of the two great epochs of mankind—that of heroes or
demi-gods and that of men [5]—a division according to which the heroic past,
notwithstanding the uniqueness inherent in its character of factual reality, had
to constitute the archetypical model for the present, almost in a perennial return to the mythical and exemplary age of the origins. This mental attitude, although recognizing the importance of chance and diversity in man's actions
and thoughts, [6] does not emphasize in a historical event what is linear,
unrepeatable and specific, but transforms it into a mythological category, according to a conception which tends to be cyclic, and which represents the
meanings and aims of human history by way of a constant relation between
present history and the mythical world of its origins. [7] It is such a polarization
which, even in the plurality of directions and tendencies, was destined to
mould Greek historical thought, and to reappear with new clarity and force in
the Roman historians of the archaic age. [8]

Within the area of this basic approach the two fundamental problems of
all ancient history are to be found: first, the problem of the causal link between
past and present, and therefore the search for causes, both remote and recent;
secondly, the problem of truth or likelihood: that is, of critical investigation as-
certaining the veracity of the information which the historian acquires from
oral transmission or written documents.

But it is just in dealing with the problem of causes [9] that the contrast between two marked tendencies in the Greek historians begins to take shape. The
legend of the Trojan war can be used by Herodotus (5th century B.C.) [10] as a
point of reference in giving reasons for the great dispute between the Greeks
and the Persians, according to the same kind of causal link already noted in
Ionic elegy, which showed that violence suffered must necessarily find recom-
pensation in an equal and opposite action. For Thucydides [11] however, the return to that distant, mythical past of the struggle between the Greeks and the
Trojans offers only a term of comparison by which to measure the greatness of
the political and military proportions of the Peloponnesian war which was
fought in his own time between the Athenians and the Spartans. Although
keeping to a structural scheme which embraces the mythical past and the actual present, Thucydides finds "the real, but unstated cause," which made the
war inevitable, at the political level, in the growing dimensions of Athenian
power which had awakened fear and apprehension in the Spartans. [12]

The discussion of truth and likelihood or probability brings the historiographic problem into the realm of the art of rhetoric and in particular of

forensic eloquence, in the sense that the historian, like the orator, must reconstruct the unfolding of events on the basis of testimony and evidence, which
confirm the credibility of the declared thesis.

We read in Thucydides: [13]

But as to the facts of the occurrences of the war, I have thought it my
duty to give them, not as ascertained from any chance informant nor as
seemed to me probable, but only after investigating with the greatest possible
accuracy each detail, in the case both of the events in which I myself partici-
pated and of those regarding which I got my information from others. And
the endeavour to ascertain these facts was a laborious task, because those
who were eye-witnesses of the several events did not give the same reports
about the same things, but reports varying according to their championship
of one side or the other, or according to their recollection. And it may well
be that the absence of the fabulous from my narrative will seem less pleasing
to the ear; but whoever shall wish to have a clear view both of the events
which have happened and of those which will some day, in all human probability, happen again in the same or a similar way—for these to adjudge my
history profitable will be enough for me. And, indeed, it has been composed, not as a prize-essay to be heard for the moment, but as a possession
for all time. [Translated by Charles Forster Smith.]

This programmatic affirmation, which expounds the criteria of a rigorous
search for truth (or liklihood, where the control of the truth is not possible) and
which lays the basis of the historiographic direction which Polybius, in the second century B.C., was to term "*apodeictic*," already had its antecedents in the
Ionic historiography of Hecataeus of Miletus (sixth-fifth centuries B.C.) who
relied on history, that is on his own experience and personal examination, for
narration of facts and the criticism of myths. [14]

Herodotus too, in setting out the results of his research (*histories apodexis*)
always distinguishes carefully between information obtained by direct observation (*opsis*) and information which he has instead derived from the chronicles
of others (*logoi*). [15] However, in the latter case, although, as he himself states, [16]
he feels the need to report what he has learned, he does not feel obliged to
believe it. [17]

In Herodotus the premises both of the criticism of tradition and the theory
of causes begin to be sketched. [18] But in Thucydides these hints of doctrine
become the object of rigid and systematic theorizing, which goes so far as absolutely to reject any element which cannot be critically controlled and to adopt
the idea of usefulness as the final aim of historical narration. The mythical and
imaginary components present in the stories of the poets and in the prose history of the logographers were thus rejected in the name of historical truth as
mere instruments of psychological pressure intended to attract the hearer. [19]

But we must ask what in Thucydides' situation motivated this radical break
with the preceding Herodotean historiography. The traditional explanation
presents the age of Thucydides as the twilight of a still "primitive" type of men-

tality, when rationality in human thinking begins to be prevalent: this level of analysis presents a naive antithesis between the mythic and the logical mentality, which it views as successive moments in the evolution of thought. Such naiveté today seems untenable in the light of modern ethnological and anthropological research.[20] The explanation, if any, is to be sought in the field of the technology of communication and information and in relation to the passage, which was under way in Thucydides' time, from an oral culture to one of written communication.[21] The analytical and rational method which Thucydides demanded in historical writing was not, in fact, applicable either to traditional poetry or to the history of logographers, because an oral culture, due to its direct, immediate relations with a listening public, has mental attitudes and means of expression which differ from those of a culture of written communication. In a predominantly oral culture there is an art of writing which, in its psychological aspect, can be said to aim, by means of clear and concrete language and through paratactic, not hypotactic, structure, at preparing attitudes of thought which are immediately perceptible to the hearer and arrest his attention. This is the stylistic structure which one meets in the fragments of Hecataeus[22] and the *Histories* of Herodotus, which were, in fact, composed for public hearing.[23] Thucydides' argument with traditional historiography, whether in poetry or in prose, appears in very precise terms in the clearly expressed criticism (I.21) against the hedonistic aim of oral narration, designed to amuse the hearer rather than for a vigorous investigation of the truth, as in his own historiography. This point of view also defines the aims and means of communication of his work, which is not composed for the brief duration of a public declamation before a passing audience, but to constitute a permanent intellectual acquisition based on the written word and careful reading.[24]

It is difficult to imagine a prose style more alien from the structural means and requirements of a public performance than that of Thucydides. Compact, compressed writing, tending to implicit rather than explicit thought, characterised by a tight, logical concatenation, it is a style which had difficulty in finding an audience disposed to follow the thread of the discourse with pleasure, requiring as it does by its very character an attentive reader alone with the text.[25]

This critical attitude with respect to oral culture can be placed on the same level as Euripides' condemnation of all the poetry of the past[26]—"gastronomic" poetry, to use a metaphor of Bertolt Brecht's—in the sense that its principal aim was that of delighting, with the pleasure of song, the public of a banquet or a formal feast, rather than the more essential one of freeing man from sorrow.[27] Later Plato's objection to the poetry of the past, analogous to the Thucydidean criticism, placed the accent exactly on the absence of a rationalistic analysis of experience and of an appropriately dialectical development of thought.[28]

A different and opposite direction, which today we would call anthropological and ethnographic, has its antecedents in Herodotus and generally in the

Ionic logographers. The assumption on which this historiography works is that the activity of the historian, like that of the dramatic poet, belongs to the sphere of mimesis, i.e. the faithful and graphic representation of human life. In the introduction to his *History*, Duris of Samos (third-second centuries B.C.),[29] arguing against his predecessors, Ephorus and Theopompus, pupils of Isocrates, because they had not known how to express the truth of the facts with sufficient efficacy, pointed out that this failure was due to their lack of interest in the mimetic aspect of narration and to the pleasure which it provoked in the public.[30] Ephorus and Theopompus, according to Duris, had pre-eminently turned their interest to the "written page" (*graphein*), ignoring all those delightful elements which spring from a kind of mimetic narration which represents, through the influence of the words (*hēdonē en tōi phrasai*), the truth of human life. In other words, they had not felt the need for a written word which could arouse in the reader the same delight which the spoken word awoke in the listener.

The nodal point of Duris' argument with the two Isocratean historians is in the distinct contrast between the spoken word (*phrasai*) and the written word (*graphein*). The meaning of Duris' categorical affirmation that Ephorus and Theopompus were concerned only with writing is clarified by Isocrates himself in a well-known passage of the *Panathenaic* where the diverse activities of speaking in public and writing are compared: if one requires particular gifts of a psychic and physical nature—courage, polemical vigour, range and strength of voice—for the other the aptitude for philosophical reflection, which can find its adequate and elaborate expression only in the assiduous act of writing, is indispensable.[31] Naturally, although Isocrates, lacking, as he himself declares, the natural, physical and psychic requirements necessary for public speaking (but perhaps also due to a deep-seated vocation), was obliged to orientate his choice towards the activity of writing. Recalling the examples of Homer and the tragic poets,[32] he recognised the validity of the spoken word and its emotional and psychagogic effects: a validity which naturally is developed at the level of delight, not at that of usefulness. But he proposed usefulness as the aim of his writing, in the sense that he tried to form an ethical-political consciousness in the reader through a rational development of the argument and the resources of a sober, flowing eloquence. This gives us elaborate writing, contrary to all psychagogic effects, but perfectly aware of its efficacy, characterized by long, solemn, harmoniously constructed sentences. As prose it is elegant and artistic, but sometimes monotonous and dull, intended mainly to scan the logical articulation of the thought with its rhythm. In short, "graphic" not "agonistic" eloquence, as Aristotle was to say, contrasting in his rhetorical doctrine the structures and functions of oral narration and the quite different ones of written narration: not intended to express emotion, more "precise," more attentive in connecting thoughts and in formal elaboration, but less alive, too narrow and sluggish for the ear.[33]

As we can see, Aristotle here is delineating a real doctrine of communication: it establishes the implicit, theoretical premise of the polemical attitude of Duris who, in fact, reproached Ephorus and Theopompus for having given to historical treatises the same bookish foundation which Isocrates' eloquence had shown.[34]

Dionysius of Halicarnassus,[35] in setting out the aspects and tendencies of Theopompus' historiography, offers precise elements of ascertainment, which confirm Duris' remarks on the bookish character of his work: the philosophical and moralizing arrangement of the narration, with frequent digressions on human virtues, long, accurate, solemn sentences, attentive to the correct balance of the images and to the rhythmic movements of the sentence, only occasionally pungent and biting, where the moralistic attitude of the writer came to censure human vices and passions.

Certainly, the psychological characterization of historical characters, the description of surroundings and customs and also of every element which arouses wonder and amazement, represent an essential component of his work, which Dionysius terms "polymorphia," and which has the primary function of usefulness rather than of psychagogic influence on the reader. It aimed, that is, at widening and deepening the knowledge of human nature.

This representational polymorphic aspect, as we have noted, also entails a type of mimetic narration, but not in the sense desired by Duris, a type of dramatic mimesis, capable of bringing the events narrated back to life, with all their emotional force, so as to transform the reader into spectator.[36] Thus the historian becomes, like the dramatic actor, the creator of a mimetic intermediary between historic reality and the public which experiences it, in a close rapport of sympathetic identification.

It is in this emotional and mimetic relation that historical *truth* appears,[37] that truth which, according to Duris, the followers of Isocrates had not been able to reach or, at least, we could say, had tried to unfold through an abstract, moral evaluation of people and events.[38] But, if the ethical truth of Theopompus had usefulness as its goal—the same educational usefulness which was the aim of the publicly orientated writing of Isocrates-Duris' mimetic truth performed the hedonistic function of arousing emotion in the reader and of pleasurably enthralling him in the narrative, a function which belonged to the spoken word.

The notion of "pleasure" or "delight" (*hēdonē*) which words, joined with dance, gesture and song, can exercise on the listener, was one of the guiding ideas of all Greek poetry from Homer to the tragedians,[39] and found its clearest and most explicit expression in the thought of Gorgias:[40]

I consider and define all poetry as speech in a metrical form. Into him who listens to it creeps a shiver of fear and compassion that induces tears and an intense desire which tends towards sorrow: before the happy and adverse fate of extraneous events and people, by the action of the words, the soul feels the emotions of others as its own . . . . The divine charm of the words awakens pleasure, banishes sorrow, identifying itself with the opinion of the soul, the power of enchantment betwitches, influences and transforms one with its magic.[41]

But this relation of emotionalism, which established itself in the performance of a poetic text, would not be understandable without the idea of mimesis, which was at the base of the Greek conception of poetic creation:[42] mimesis as a bringing back to life through words, music, gesture and dancing, of a mythical or human action or a natural phenomenon. A mimetic process which transmits itself to the listener under the form of emotional participation.

But if pleasure becomes as one with emotionalism, which in its turn is related to mimesis, it follows that pleasure is one of the aspects or functions of mimesis itself. The relationship is clear from Aristotle's declaration on tragic poetry: "The (tragic) poet must procure, by means of mimesis, the pleasure which pity and fear arouse."[43]

It is clear then that "the pleasure inherent in utterance" (*hēdonē en tói phrasai*) of which Duris speaks does not belong to the mere artifice of style which, on the contrary, characterizes the technique of composition directed only to the written word, but to the efficacy of the spoken word, in that it is the vehicle of expression for the mimetic message. In essence, Duris underlined the necessity for the written page to preserve the dramatic tension and concentration of the tragic performance—an undoubted transposition of tragic mimesis into the area of historical narrative. In this sense Duris is certainly traveling in the wake of Aristotle's *Poetics*, but with different theoretical connotations, in that he tends to identify the activities of the poet and historian in their means and aims which, on the contrary, Aristotle[44] vigorously distinguishes, assigning to the first the task of narrating the "general" or what could happen according to likelihood and necessity, to the second the "particular"—what has really happened. But, once this identification of the two activities of poet and historian is declared, it is clear that the identification implicitly brings in its train a need that history too should have the category of the "general," which is, in fact, for Duris the mimetic *truth*, as a dramatic concentration of human passions.[45]

In this antimony, between history as an account of the particular and history as individualisation of the general, are defined, in terms which today are still current, the duties of the historian as regards the facts, that is the problem of the particular and the general, of objectivity and subjectivity, which is as much as to say the dialectical relation between facts and their interpretation.

This use of history, outside its complex, doctrinal relations with Aristotelism, had deep motivations in the cultural reality of the fourth-third centuries B.C. and precisely in the expressionistic tendencies of figurative art[46] and new forms of entertainment, that is the new dithyramb and solo-singing. The expressionistic mimetism of the new poetry and music is clearly outlined, even in its technical aspects and causes, in the pseudo-Aristotelian *Problems*;[47] the introduction of solo-singing, without strophes, in contrast with the strophic structure of the chorus, and relying on the technical ability of a new type of professional actor, responded to the new need to express human passions in their authentic truth, no longer within the limits of that "conventional character" which had marked choral singing in fifth century theatre. With its tendency for psychological analysis of the characters and a type of ethnographic investigation, mimetic historiography found also a suitable background in the political life of the Hellenistic courts of the Diadochi characterized by the determining influence of the personalities of the rulers and princes[48] and the view of the multiform world of the non-Greek populations of the Hellenized Orient.

But, in fact, in the contrasts of such a way of elaborating historical "truth," intended to represent human life dramatically in all its baffling complexity, resurface those very methodological instances of a rigorous, objective search for the facts and their causes which, as we have seen, had characterized Thucydides' historical thought. These are the terms of Polybius' (second century B.C.) bitter polemic against Phylarchus, a follower of Duris' historiographical idea, concerning his dramatic account of the fall of Mantinea:[49]

In his eagerness to arouse the pity and attention of his readers (*sympatheis poiein*) he (Phylarchus) treats us to a picture of clinging women with their hair dishevelled and their breasts bare, or again of crowds of both sexes together with their children and aged parents weeping and lamenting as they are led away to slavery. This sort of thing he keeps up throughout his history, always trying to bring horrors vividly before our eyes. Leaving aside the ignoble and womanish character of such a treatment of his subject, let us consider how far it is proper or serviceable to history. A historical author should not try to thrill his readers by such exaggerated pictures, nor should he, like a tragic poet, try to imagine the probable utterances of his characters or reckon up all the consequences probably incidental to the occurrences with which he deals, but simply record what really happened and what really was said, however commonplace. For the object of tragedy is not the same as that of history, but quite the opposite. The tragic poet should thrill and charm his audience for the moment by the verisimilitude of the words he puts into his characters' mouths, but it is the task of the historian to instruct and convince for all time serious students by the truth of the facts and the speeches he narrates, since in the one case it is the probable that takes precedence, even if it be untrue, the purpose being to create illusion in spectators, in the other it is the truth, the purpose being to confer benefit on learners. Apart from this, Phylarchus simply narrates most of such catastrophes and does not even suggest their causes or the nature of these causes, without which it is impossible in any case to feel either legitimate pity or proper anger. [Translated by W.R.Paton.]

This page of Polybius forces itself on the attention not only for its polemical content but above all for the lucid synthesis in which he groups together all the theoretical aspects of the long debate on history as mimesis or as a critical investigation, as art or as "science." The antimony between tragedy and history is to be seen in an elaborate system of semantics belonging to different means of communication and information, and thus to different thought structures and the different functions of the two types of narration. To the ideas (belonging to poetry in its oral contact with a listening public) of emotional participation (*sympatheia*), illusion, likelihood, pleasure and momentariness, is opposed the truth, the usefulness and permanence of historical research which urges the intellectual diligence of the reader. It is a critical basis on which are united doctrinal motives already observed in Gorgias, Thucydides and in Aristotle and which confirms the sense of antithesis worked out by Duris between the spoken word (*phrasai*) and the written word (*graphein*).[50]

It is evident that this historiography, as it aimed at a comprehensive representation of life in its multiple and varied characters, situations, etc., must necessarily have appeared to Polybius as lacking in that rigorous, unequivocal method which was the premise of his "pragmatic" and "apodeictic" history.

It is, therefore, a historiography "without method," this of Duris and Phylarchus, to which must undoubtedly be related the theory of Tauriscus,[51] Crates' pupil, on the unsystematic character of the *historikon* or "historian" who deals with the *amethodos hylē*, "a disordered matter," that is precisely a complex and multiform subject which is not susceptible to a controlled analysis by precise, methodical standards.[52]

But it is just this absence of an unequivocal method, or at least of the method of Polybian historiography, together with the vitality of the existential content and the multiplicity of human interests which deprived this historiographical direction of reputation and reliability, so that it ended by being misunderstood even by the ancient critics[53] as a decadent tendency towards romantic invention.

Plutarch's comment on the reliability of Duris' account of the return of Alcibiades to Athens is typical:[54]

Duris the Samian, who claims that he was a descendant of Alcibiades, gives some additional details. He says that the oarsmen of Alcibiades rowed to the music of a flute blown by Chrysogonus the Pythian victor; that they kept time to a rhythmic call from the lips of Callippides, the tragic actor; that both these artists were arrayed in the long tunics, flowing robes and other adornment of their profession; and that the commander's ship put into harbours with a sail of purple hue, as though, after a drinking bout, he were off on a revel. But neither Theopompus, nor Ephorus, nor Xenophon mentions these things, nor is it likely that Alcibiades put on such airs for the Athenians, to whom he was returning after he had suffered exile and many great adversities. Nay, he was in actual fear as he put into the harbour, and once in, he did not leave his trireme until, as he stood on deck, he caught sight of his cousin Euryptolemus on shore, with many other friends and kinsmen, and heard their cries of welcome. [Translated by Bernadette Perrin.]

But whatever weight we may give to Plutarch's judgement, always so much against Duris' historiography,[55] it is a fact that the representation of the scene, in all its theatrical solemnity and ostentation, is within the dimensions of the character, his ways and attitudes, as we can see from the biography of Plutarch himself.[56] In essence this mimetic historiography, in the importance which it gives to every aspect of human behaviour together with the individualization even of its irrational components, contained in itself deep implicit needs which we today would call ethnological, psychological and sociological. It was an expressionistic historiography which, outside the methodological limits of a strictly political historiography, tended to represent directly the face of life. If its approach was alien to the aim of usefulness in a Thucydidean sense or the moralizing and philosophic usefulness of the Isocrateans, even it, however, followed a precise propaedeutic aim which is implicit, according to Aristotle, in the *tragic* representation of the passions.

But the contrast between the two types of historiography operated at the level more of programmatic intentions and expressions than of narrative procedure, if one considers the numerous indications of dramatic representations in those very historians, such as Thucydides and Polybius, who, from a theoretical point of view, rejected any concession to a hedonistic and psychagogic use of history.[57]

In the critical view which we have outlined here, we would like to emphasize the need for a revaluation of this historiography, above all now that contemporary thought, even with the assistance of new methodology and techniques of investigation, has reopened the debate on what history is and on the task of the historian.[58]

Polybius' polemic did not exhaust itself in the contrast between his own method of historical investigation and mimetically orientated historiography: no less bitterly and more widely, with precise, critical interventions on method and contents, it attacked above all the Isocratean historiographic orientation, represented, as we have seen, by Ephorus and Theopompus. In the introduction to book IX of his *Histories*, Polybius, once again with severity and clarity, expounds the principles which distinguish his historiographical point of view from the predominant Isocratean one:

> I am not unaware that my work, owing to the uniformity of its composition, has a certain severity, and will suit the taste and gain the approval of only one class of reader. For nearly all other writers, or at least most of them, by dealing with every branch of history, attract many kinds of people to the perusal of their works. The genealogical side appeals to those who are fond of a story, and the account of colonies, the foundation of cities, and their ties of kindred, such as we find, for instance, in Ephorus, attracts the curious and lovers of recondite lore, while the student of politics is interested in the doings of nations, cities and monarchs. As I have confined my attention strictly to these last matters and as my whole work treats of nothing else, it is, as I say, adapted to only one sort of reader, and its perusal will have no attractions for the larger number. [Translated by W.R.Paton.]

Thus, Polybius' history is esentially "pragmatic," limited, that is, by political events and excluding any discussion of an ethnographic or anthropological type which pertains to legendary traditions and to the founding of cities and colonies,[59] those very events preferred above all by the Isocratean type of historian. It is an account which concentrates completely on the stating of contemporary facts and is thus always new and always different, since it does not deal with the past, but with the present and, consequently, cannot draw on the statements of preceding historiographical models.[60] In defining the aim of his method of working, Polybius follows in the wake of Thucydides with a rigid contrast between the usefulness (*ophelimon*) of his own history and the pleasure (*terpsis*) which Isocratean historiography arouses in its readers.

But the terms of this polemic are specified with greater vividness and documentation in the very part of his work where he subjects to sharp criticism the work of his great predecessor, Timaeus of Tauromenium (fourth-third centuries B.C.) who had related the adventures of the Greek West down to the beginning of the first Punic War: just where, in fact, Polybius' narrative began. The dominant themes of Timaeus' work, as can be deduced from the critical writings of Polybius himself, were the same as those which had characterized Isocratean historiography: colonies, founding of cities, relationships, family histories, geographical digressions and the customs of different peoples.[61] That Timaeus' writings were characterized by Isocratean rules is explicitly stated by Dionysius of Halicarnassus[62] and indirectly confirmed by the judgment of Cicero on their "graphic" and not "agonistic" character,[63] a point which is precisely verified in Duris' polemic against Ephorus and Theopompus whose interest was in *graphein* rather than *phrasai*.[64]

But other elements of structure and form also bring Timaeus back to the Isocratean way, through the frigidity of his writing, the prolixity of his account and that marked tendency towards philosophical reflection and sententious aphoristic language[65] which Polybius[66] bitterly censured, not so much for its aprioristic foreclosing as for a claimed superficiality or speculative incapacity on the part of Timaeus.

But, leaving aside every other aspect of Polybius' polemic on real or presumed historical and geographical errors,[67] our aim is now to examine his basic objection to the bias inherent in the attitude of Timaeus' historical writings which mirrored the essentially propagandist aim of Isocratean publicity. This use of history tends to demonstrate a thesis and operates, therefore, like oratory, with the criterion of "probability" and not with the criterion of the truth, that is, that "truth" without which history, according to Polybius, becomes a vain and useless narrative.[68]

In fact, Polybius, from his point of view, accuses Timaeus of falsifying historical truth not only due to the lack of direct knowledge of the places he deals with, the bookish attitude of his work, and because he has no real experience of any form of activity, public or private,[69] but also and above all because he deliberately lies. Thus, with reference to Locri Epizephirii he observes, in the manipulation of the facts, that probability is a simple trick to disguise wilful lies:[70]

Timaeus frequently makes false statements. He appears to me not to be in general uninformed about such matters, but his judgment to be darkened by prejudice; and when he once sets himself to blame or praise anyone he forgets everything and departs very widely from his duty as a historian . . . I am even ready to concede that Timaeus' account is more probable [than Aristotle's one]. But is this a reason why a historical writer whose statements seem lacking in probability must submit to listen to every term of contumely and almost to be put on trial for his life? Surely not. For those, as I said, who make false statements owing to error should meet with kind correction and forgiveness, but those who lie deliberately deserve an implacable accuser. [Translated by W.R. Paton.]

But the discussion on truth and likelihood still merits some comments. If Ephorus had denied that epideictic oratory required more attention, diligence and preparation than historical works,[71] Timaeus, specifying the terms of this distinction, put the accent on the superiority of history with an analogical argument[72] which clearly presupposes the Platonic theory of two different levels of mimesis in the field of man's artisan and artistic activities: the artisan, in constructing any object, uses a direct imitation of the idea of the object itself; the artist, be he painter, sculptor or poet, in finding the contents of his artistic function, makes, in his turn, an imitation of an imitation, that is, he reproduces the object of an artisan which is itself the reproduction of an idea.[73] For Timaeus there is an identical relationship between historical and epideictic narrative, which he compares respectively to the real constructions and furnishings which are the work of the artisan, and to the figurative constructions and furnishings in pictorial art. This is an argument conducted along the lines of the distinction between one mimesis as a perfect reproduction of reality and a second mimesis which, like sketch (skiagraphia)[74] and scene-painting,[75] creates a perspective illusion by deforming reality, in that distant objects are represented as being small and the nearer ones as large: an art, this, of illusion, that is to say, an art of deceptive likelihood.

But this scheme of argumentation, according to Polybius, turns back against Timaeus, since faithful reproduction of reality could not consist, as he declared, in the onerous task of the collection and study of the sources necessary for his historical narration, but rather in direct acquaintance with the places and personal experience of the situations[76]:

In my opinion the difference between real buildings and scene-paintings or between history and declamatory speech-making is not so great as is, in the case of all works, the difference between an account founded on participation, active or passive, in the occurrences and one composed from report and the narratives of others. [Translated by W.R. Paton]

Exactly in Timaeus' bookish technique of constructing a historical argument Polybius recognizes a reason even for involuntary errors; and on the occasion when Timaeus approaches the truth it is always an artificial rather than real truth. He works like "those painters who reproduce straw models": their exterior design coincides with the real one, but is not capable of rendering the vitality and animation of living creatures.[77]

On the contrary, a historiography which wishes to adhere doggedly to the truth of the events which it relates must, according to Polybius,[78] respond to three fundamental methodological requirements: the careful study and critical analysis of the documents, a visit to the places in question (*autopsia*), a direct knowledge of the political problems. It is a "pragmatic" (*pragmatiké*) historiography in content, inasmuch as its subjects are the political, military and other events of recent and contemporary history, "apodeictic" (*apodeiktikē*) in its method, in that it proceeds according to the principles of "scientific" demonstration.[79]

Two opposite uses of history which are both aimed at the preparation of a man of politics, but in different ways and at different levels: one, that of the Isocratean proposing precise political and cultural objectives to be pursued; the other furnishing all the rigorously tested tools of political craft, of which the politician must be aware when making decisions, if he is to avoid falling into the errors committed in the past. The first is a partisan or propagandistic historiography and in this sense it too is faithful to a reality,[80] the second programmatically "impartial" and "objective," not politically involved, precisely because it is orientated towards the elaboration of a useful technique for politicians whatever their particular and incidental aims may be.

(We wish to thank Dr. David Murray who translated this article and Prof. John Van Sickle who also advised on some technical points of translation.)

NOTES AND REFERENCES

[1] Original title: "Strutture comunicative del discorso storico nel pensiero storiografico dei Greci", published in *Il Verri*, giugno 1973, pp. 53–78. *Le teorie del discorso storico nel pensiero greco e la storiografia romana arcaica*, Rome 1975, pp. 17–45.

[2] Cf. S. Mazzarino, *Il pensiero storico classico* I, Bari 1966, p. 38 ff.

[3] Fr. 12D. 9 West: Cf. S. Mazzarino, *loc. cit.*

[4] For a fuller treatment see B. Gentili, 'Lirica greca arcaica e tardo-arcaica', in *Introduzione allo studio della cultura classica*, Milano, 1972 p. 57 ff.

[5] Hom. *Il.* 12,23; Hes. *Op.* 160; frr. 1; 204, 97 ff. Merk.-West. Cf. K. Latte, in *Histoire et historiens dans l'antiquité*, Entret. Hardt IV, 1956, p. 3 f.

[6] One may think of the notion of chance (*symphorē, tychē*), which recurs in the Greek historians and, for the idea of diversity, that is that "no day produces one event similar to another" or that the thoughts of men are always changing, see Herodt. 1, 32;

Archil. frr. 131–132 West = 107–108 Tard.; Pind. *Nem.* 6, 6, Pyth. 8, 95 ff. On the sense of *ephameroi* ("beings who change opinion every day") in the last two citations, cf. H. Fränkel, *Wege und Formen frühgriech. Denkens*, München 1960², p. 23 ff.

[7] It is not opportune to go back to the old argument about the conception of time in classical historiography. It is certain that excessively rigid schematizing led to the idea of a sharp contrast between the cyclic conception of time in Greek thought and the linear conception of the Judeo-Christian cultural tradition, which is not corroborated by the complexity of attitudes of ancient thought. In fact, with the idea of "Historical Return" one sometimes associates even ideas relative to the evolutionary process; and above all the concept of "Return" does not imply complete similarity between historical events, but rather exemplarity, in the sense of "Return" to a mythical models in individual or collective behaviour and attitude. For a balanced and exhaustive reexamination of the problem cf. S. Mazzarino, *Il pensiero storico classico* II 2, p.412 ff.

[8] The idea of origin still lives, although within the limits of a different conception of history, no longer cyclic but horizontal, in medieval Christian historiography. In particular, as far as regards the chronicles of single cities, cf. A. Carile, "Le origini della societá veneziana nella storiografia locale" in G. Folena, *Storia della cultura veneta* I 4 (in the press).

[9] "Causes" in the most obvious sense, in the sphere of a deterministic conception to which certain subtle distinctions of contemporary historiography, which substitutes the idea of "cause" with that of "function", are foreign. In other words, more than the problem of "why", we today are inclined to pose that of "how" a given event is inserted in the internal logic of the situation. For more details on the concept of historical causality today see E. H. Carr, *What is History?*, London 1961, c.IV. On the idea of function and purpose which, in all sectors of contemporary culture, is substituting that of causality, cf. V. Therrien, *La révolution de Gaston Bachelard en critique littéraire. Ses fondements, ses techniques, sa portée. Du nouvel esprit scientifique à un nouvel esprit littéraire*, Paris 1970, p.123 f.

[10] 1. 1–5

[11] 1, 9–11

[12] 1,23,6

[13] 1, 22, 2–4

[14] Cf. *F.Gr.Hist.* 1 F 1; see Latte, *art.cit.* p.5

[15] 2, 99

[16] 7, 152

[17] On the problem of sight and hearing as sources of historical information, see especially G. Nenci, "Il motivo dell'autopsia nella storiografica greca", *Studi classici e orientali* 3, 1953, p.14 ff; M. Laffranque, *Rev.philos.* 1963, p.75 ff.; 1968, p.263 ff. The question deserves re-examination to put it in closer relationship with the evolution of the technology of communication from the oral and aural phase to that of the production and diffusion of books.

[18] Herodotus distinguishes between *prophasis* (the declared motive, the pretext), *aitia* (the real motive) and *arche* (the occasion, initial moment of a military or political event): cf. J. L. Myres, *Herodotus Father of History*, Oxford 1953, p.56.

[19] 1, 21, 1

[20] Cf. B. Gentili, "L'interpretazione dei lirici greci arcaici nella dimensione del nostro tempo. Sincronia e diacronia nello studio di una cultura orale," *Quad.Urb.* 8, 1969, p.20 f.; "Lirica greca arcaica" *cit.* p.62 ff.

21 Cf. E. G. Turner, *Athenian Books in the Fifth and Fourth Centuries B.C.*, London 1952; E. A. Havelock, *Preface to Plato*, Oxford 1963; B. Gentili, *artt. citt.*; G. Cavallo, *Scriptorium* 26, 1972, p. 71 f.

22 Cf. K. Latte, *art. cit.* p. 5

23 For a correct interpretation of the ancient evidence for the public readings held by Herodotus at Athens and Olympia, cf. L. Canfora, 'Il *ciclo* storico,' *Belfagor* 26, 1971, p. 659 f.

24 This is the sense of "my history is a permanent possession (*ktēma eis aei*) not a recital (*agonisma*) intended for the momentary listener." The word *ktēma* is not only and exclusively a metaphor, but preserves the normal meaning of "property" in a concrete sense which is referable to any object, the possession of which is lasting and inalienable. But if such is the value of *ktēma*, its direct contrast with *agonisma*, which is the performance presented with the aim of obtaining success before a public, induces one to think that the account here deals with the opposition between the transient *hic et nunc* of the performance and the lasting existence of the account consigned to the materiality of the written word, that is the book: cf. T. Kleberg, *Buchhandel und Verlagswesen in der Antike*, Darmstadt 1967, p. 4 f. Certainly, Thucydides, as has been shown (L. Canfora, *art. cit.*, p. 657), foresaw (1,22,4) that his work would be read in public performances, according to the traditional practice; but the important fact is that he was not interested so much in the moment of the performance, as in the usefulness (*loc. cit.*) of his rational account to those who, in the future, would learn by reading it. The term *ktēma*, referring to the material property of the book, has a significant comparison in the use of the Latin *monumentum*, which could mean any monument in stone or bronze, but also a literary work in prose or verse, in the materiality of its written terms: cf. among the many examples Cato fr. 83 Peter; Cic. *De or.* 1,46,201; Hor. *Carm* 3,30,1; Quint. 12,10,51.

25 Dion. Hal. *De comp. verb.* 22,II p. 108 Us.–Rad. explicitly affirms that Thucydidean prose does not respond to the requirements of a text intended for public recitation.

26 *Med.* 190 ff.

27 For more details cf. B. Gentili, 'Lirica greca arcaica,' *cit.* p. 63

28 It has been the special merit of E. A. Havelock (*op. cit.*) to have clarified in a definitive way that Plato's criticism of traditional poetry expresses the requirements of the new culture of written communication which was asserting itself in the second half of the fifth century B.C. In this sense Euripides, Thucydides and Plato are the bearers of a single, identical cultural message. All three place at the center of their polemical propositions the rigid contrast between the usefulness (*ophelimon*) of a rational account, and the pleasure (*hēdonē, terpein*), inherent in the practice of the performance. Thus for the first time that antinomy between the useful and the delightful, which was destined to remain one of the typical characteristics of European culture, was outlined (cf. E. A. Havelock, *op. cit.* p. 157 f.)

29 *F. Gr. Hist.* 76 F1.

30 The meaning of Duris' formulation is clarified by a passage of Diodorus (20,43,7), from which it is evident that: 1) the aim of "mimesis" is the representation of the "truth" of the facts and of the pathos inherent in them; 2) a historical account without pathos, which is the very substance of the facts, is, to be sure, still an "imitation," but one which falls short of the "truth." On the undoubted dependence of this theoretical declaration on Duris, cf. Ed. Schwartz, *R. E.* s. v. 'Diod.', col. 687; s. v. 'Duris', col. 1855. The argument of Diodorus (Duris) regards the concept of the inadequacy of

historical narrative, in that different actions which happened simultaneously are presented in an "unnatural" time sequence and not in their simultaneousness: therefore, an account which does not represent the truth of the situations in an authentic way. For more details cf. H. Strasburger, *Die Wesensbestimmung der Geschichte durch die antike Geschichtsschreibung*, Wiesbaden 1968[2], pp. 79 and 85.

[31] 12, 10–11

[32] 2,48 f.

[33] *Rhet.* 3, 1413 b ff.

[34] In fact it is not possible to understand Duris' formulation, in all the implications which pertain to the foundation of the historical narrative and its formal aspects, if we leave aside the antithesis *phrasai-graphein* and the exact meaning of *graphein*, which raises the whole problem of communication technology and the terms in which it was explicitly described, as we have seen, by the culture of the fourth century B.C. This requirement, up to now, does not seem to have been noticed by the critics and, even when attention has been paid to the value of *graphein*, as in the recent analysis, quite penetrating on other points, by Strasburger (*op. cit.*, p. 79 ff.), the word has been interpreted in a more formal than substantial key, in the exterior sense of "style"; since *graphein*, in the meaning elaborated by Isocrates and Aristotle, takes in not only the argument of rhetorical figures and tropes, but the very structures of thought, in relation to the exact requirements of written communication.

[35] *Epist. ad Pomp.* 6, II p. 244 ff. US.–Rad. =*F. Gr. Hist.* 115 T 20.

[36] B. L. Ullman, "History and Tragedy", *Trans. Am. Philol. Ass.* 73, 1942, pp. 25 ff., is right in recognising already in Theopompus a form of dramatization of history and, therefore, the introduction to a type of mimetic historiography, but he is wrong in thinking that Duris' orientation is the direct continuation of that of the Isocrateans Ephorus and Theopompus. Apart from some apparent convergences, which meet in their common ethnographical and biographical interests, the nodal point of the divergence is precisely in the different meaning and function which the idea of mimesis assumes in Duris' historiographic thought and practice. Cf. the remarks made by K. von Fritz on Ullman's thesis in *Histoire et historiens dans l'antiquité*, Entret. Hardt IV, 1956, p. 126 ff.

[37] Cf. n. 30

[38] Cf. Dion. Hal. *loc. cit.*

[39] The frequence of textual references does not here permit an exhaustive documentation. It is sufficient to examine I. Latacz, *Zum Wortfeld "Freude" in der Sprache Homers*, Heidelberg 1966 and, more especially, E. A. Havelock, *op. cit.* p. 152 ff. and *passim*.

[40] B 11,9 f. D-K. (II, p. 230,20)

[41] Regarding tragic "performance," Gorgias insists on the idea of the illusion exercised on the audience by poetry, presenting it as a mutual emotional rapport between the poet and the spectator: "he who deceives is *more just* than he who does not, and he who lets himself be deceived is *wiser* than he who does not." (B 23 D-K., ii p. 305,26). To understand the sense of this declaration, until now not completely understood, we must keep in mind that *dike* and *dikaios* ("justice" and "just") both at a cosmological level (cf. G. Vlastos, Equality and Justice in Early Greek Cosmologies *Class. Philol.* 42, 1947, p. 168 ff; L. Sambursky, *The Physical World of the Greeks*, London 1956, p. 8; J.-P. Vernant, Structure géométrique et notions politiques dans la cosmologie d'Anaximandre, *Eirene* 7, 1968, p. 5 ff.) and at an

amorous level (cf.B.Gentili, 'Il "letto insaziato" di Medea e il tema dell'*adikia* a livello amoroso nei lirici (Saffo, Teognide) e nella Medea di Euripide', *Studi classici e orientali* 1972, p.500) imply the precise idea of equilibrium in the relationship of reciprocal actions amongst natural or human agents. The violation of this principle, in that it upsets a balance, is symbolized as an act of injustice (*adikia*), which necessarily brings a punishment intended to re-establish the norm of *dikē*. The "wisdom" of him who lets himself be deceived, that is, the public, spectators, is in his capacity to put himself on the same level as the poet and to take part emotionally in the situation proposed by the performance. The terms *sophia-sophos* still preserve in Gorgias the meaning of "ability," "capacity", "experience of an art," in this case the poetic art.

[42] Cf.E.A.Havelock, *op.cit.*p.20 ff.; B.Gentili, 'I frr.39 e 40 P.di Alcmane e la poetica della mimesi nella cultura greca arcaica', *Studi in onore di Vittorio De Falco*, Napoli 1971, p.57 ff.

[43] *Poet.* 1453b; cf.also Plato *Resp.* 10,602c–608a.

[44] *Poet.* 1451a–b

[45] Von Fritz (*art.cit.*, p.107 ff.) has the merit of having clarified in what sense the Aristotelean category of the general, inherent in tragic mimesis, operated on the thought of Duris, who was Theophratus' pupil: in substance he has restricted Schwartz's thesis concerning Duris' dependence on Aristotle to clear and precise limits. The most debated problem (cf.e.g. F.Wehrli, 'Der erhabene und der schlichte Stil in der poetisch-rhetorischen Theorie der Antike', *Phyllobolia für P.von der Mühll*, Basel 1946, p.9 ff., and 'Die Geschichtsschreibung im Lichte der antiken Theorie', *Eumusia, Festgabe für E.Howald*, Zürich 1947, p.54 ff. = *Theorie und Humanitas, Gesamm.Schrift.z.antik.Gedankenwelt*, Zürich und München 1972, pp.97–120; 132–144), if the program of Duris reflects the thought of Aristotle or Isocrates, is in reality, as F.W.Walbank has rightly commented ('Tragic History. A Reconsideration', *Bull. Inst. Class. Stud. Univ. London*, 1955, p.4 ff.), a false problem, characterized by a non-critical schematism. As we have shown, the question is not posed in terms of the alternative, Aristotle or Isocrates, but in the more concrete terms of a problem with many complex cultural implications.

[46] One thinks, for example, of the famous mosaic of Alexander which depicts a battle between Macedonians and Persians (probably the battle of Isso), found at Pompei in the House of the Faun, now in the National Museum of Naples: a grandiose picture full of foreshortenings and efforts of colour, in which emerge, in a powerful dramatic concentration which does not neglect any detail of the scene, the psychological and emotive attitudes and reactions of the individual characters. Cf.Ippel, *Röm.Mitt.*45 1930, p.80 ff; Rizzo, *Pittura ellenestico-romana*, figg. 44–47; Lippold,*Gemälde Kopien*, figg. 16,86; R.Bianchi Bandinelli, *Storicitá dell' arte classica*, Firenze 1950², p. 192; *Il problema della pittura antica. Grecia classica ed etá' ellenistica e romana*. Lezioni del corso di archeologica raccolte da E. Faini, Firenze s.d., p. 100 ff.

[47] XIX 15

[48] Cf.K.Latte in his discussion on the essay of K.von Fritz in *Entret.Hardt.* IV, 1956, pp.129 f. It is clear that underlining these cultural and political implications does not mean underestimating (R.Syme on the observations of Latte in *Entret.cit.* p.132) the influence of Aristotelean theory on mimetic historiography. It is clear, even obvious, that no doctrine exercises *sic et simpliciter* its influence, without a cultural support which motivates its application and function.

[49] 2,56

[50] It is to be noted that until now the importance of Polybius' passage, for the clear understanding of the *phrasai-graphein* antithesis, has not been adequately valued.

[51] *Ap.* Sext.Emp.*Adv.math.* 1,252 f. = fr. 18 Mette, *Sphairopoiia*, München 1936.

[52] In the passage, to which Sextus Empiricus refers, Tauriscus illustrates the three moments in which, in his opinion, the activity of literary critic is articulated: "logic," regarding the lexicon and grammatical tropes, "stylistics," on dialects and styles, and finally *historikon*, on the contents of poetry and their mythological, historical, geographical and biographical implications—a subject for study, according to him, which cannot be reduced to a system, because, unlike language, it is not governed by methodical rules. It is the main merit of S.Mazzarino, *op.cit.*, I, p.484 ff. to have illustrated the implicit contrast between the Tauriscean conception of history and the apodeictic one theorized by Polybius.

[53] Cf.E.Schwartz, *R.E. s.v.* 'Duris', col.1855 f.

[54] *Alcib.* 32 = *F.Gr.Hist.* 76 F 70.

[55] Cf.*Per.* 28 (= *F.Gr.Hist.* 76 F 67) where the account of Duris of the taking of Samos by the Athenians is defined as false and tendentious.

[56] Plutarch affirms, as we have seen, that the particulars reported by Duris are not reliable, also because they are not verified in Theopompus, Ephorus and Xenophon, the other historians who related the account of Alcinbiades' return to Athens. In fact the argument is without value: precisely because Theopompus, Ephorus and Xenophon did not follow a mimetic type of historiography, they considered irrelevant certain particulars which had, on the contrary, great importance for Duris. Duris' account is confirmed by, amongst others, the fairly similar one of Athenaeus 12, 535 C–D.

[57] See Strasburger, *op.cit.* p.80 ff. and recently J. Percival, 'Thucydides and the Uses of History', *Greece and Rome* 1971, p.199 ff.

[58] Cf.P.Veyne, *Comment on écrit l'histoire. Essai d'épistémiologie*, Paris 1971. Veyne's theses, sometimes debatable and in some cases even paradoxical, are, nevertheless, stimulating and in a certain sense even provocative by the extent to which they challenge the conception of history as a science and the possibility of enucleating a real, precise historiographic method. Certainly, a very interesting position, but equally risky, at least in the terms in which it is defined by the author. When he declares that "ideas, theories and conceptions of history are unfailingly the dead part of a historical work" (p.144), he seems to want to relaunch, in essence, a certain model (which really is dead) of erudite and positivistic historiography.

[59] Pol. 9,2

[60] Pol. *ibid.*

[61] Pol. 12, 26 d On Timaeus, see A. Momigliano, *Terzo contributo alla storia degli studi classici e del mondo antico* I, Roma 1966, p.23 ff. (with bibliography).

[62] *De Din.* 8=*F.Gr.Hist.* 566 T22.

[63] *De or.* 2,14,58=*F.Gr.Hist.* 566 T20: magnam eloquentiam ad scribendum attulit sed nullum usum forensum.

[64] Cf. p. 78 f.

[65] *Cic.Brut.* 95,325 = *F.Gr.Hist.* 566 T.21; Dionys.Hal.*loc.cit.*; Anon.*De Subl.* 4 = *F.Gr.Hist.* 566 T 23.

[66] 12,25,6

[67] 12,3 ff.

[68] Pol.1,14; cf.12,12. For a precise and lucid analysis of the Isocrateanism implicit in

Timaeus' "tendentiousness", see M.A.Levi, 'La critica di Polibio a Timeo', *Miscella-nea di studi alessandrini in memoria di* A.Rostagni, Torino 1963, p.195 ff.

[69] Pol.12,25d,e,g,h; 27; 28

[70] 12,7

[71] *Ap*. Pol. 12,28,8–9= *F.Gr.Hist.*70F 111

[72] *Ap*. Pol. 12,28a= *F.Gr.Hist.* 566 F 7

[73] Plat.*Resp.*10,597 ff.; 602c; *Soph.* 233b ff.

[74] Plat.*Resp.*10.602d

[75] Tim.*loc.cit.*n.72

[76] 12,28a, 6

[77] 12,25h

[78] 12,25e

[79] It is necessary here to specify that the current use of the term "pragmatic" in the criticism of ancient historical thought is often equivocal: an equivocation which comes from the incorrect opinion that *"pragmatikos"* and*"pragmatike historia"* imply methodological types of connotation in the work of Polybius (M.Gelzer, *Festschrift C.Weickert*, Berlin 1955, p.87 ff. =*Kl.Schriften* p.155 ff.; cf. recently K.-E.Petzold, *Studien zur Methode der Polybios u. zu ihrer historischen Auswertung*, München 1969, p. 3 ff.1. In fact, a semantic analysis, which is obviously impossible here, confirms the interpretation proposed by Balsdon (*Class. Quart.* 1953, p.158 ff.), by Walbank (A *Historical Commentary on Polybius* I, Oxford 1957, pp.8, n.6; 42) and by Pédech (*La méthode historique de Polybe*, Paris 1964, p.21 ff.), according to which *"pragmatikē historia"* describes, in Polybius, the history of political and military facts, in contrast with those of genealogy, foundings of cities, colonization, etc.; that is, it regards only the contents not the attitude of historical narrative. In this second sense Polybius uses the expression *apodeiktike historia* about history which conforms to the rigid principles of a demonstrative method. For further details on historical method and polemics in Polybius, see D.Musti, 'Polibio negli studi dell'ultimo ventennio (1950–1970)' in *Aufstieg und Niedergang der Röm. Welt* I, (J. Vogt gewid.) Berlin-New York 1972, pp.1114–1181.

[80] We are not, therefore, in agreement with certain tendencies in criticism, which reduce Timaeus' historiography and in general that of the Isocrateans to a simple historiography of erudite intellectuals, totally free from political intentions.

Index